Fulfilled Through Fear

"Although many do not understand this, fear is not always the wrong response in life. A holy and reverential fear of God, in fact, is needed for a godly and fulfilling life. This biblical, wise, and well written book by a veteran Christian minister and defender of the faith can do much to make us aware that the fear of the lord is the beginning of wisdom."

—**Douglas Groothuis**, Distinguished University Research Professor of Apologetics and Christian Worldview, Cornerstone University

"As Paul Ricoeur insisted, the self knows itself only through others. If so, we know our true selves only through our Ultimate Other—God. This excellent book by Dean Halverson is both an eloquent reminder of this truth and a clarion call to seek and know God unreservedly, without whom we are but poor and tragic imitations of all that God wants us to be. Highly recommended!"

—**See Seng Tan**, President, International Students Inc.

"Whether you believe in God or not, this book is a must-read! Dean presents a counterintuitive argument that we are ultimately and overwhelmingly fulfilled not by success, comfort, or even self-awareness but through fear of the infinite and dangerous God. Can this be true? Read and find out!"

—**Darrell Dooyema**, Director, Global Commerce

"Dean Halverson has the gift of taking challenging aspects of the scriptures and making them understandable. For those seeking truth, and more specifically, understanding of the fear of God, Dean's book will bring clarity. As in other works Dean has written, his work is engaging, formative, and exhaustive in that he leaves the reader with a clear understanding of topic, with a clear understanding of what the next step could be."

—**Karl Garcia**, Pastor, Clear Creek Community Church, Texas

"In the first conversation I had with Dean Halverson, over twenty-five years ago, I was immediately struck by his profound reverence for God. That passion to truly know God remains an illuminating flame that Dean now shares with us in *Fulfilled Through Fear*. His insights have helped me not only revere God but also desire to be 'overwhelmed by God.' They will do the same for you."

—**Craig Glass**, Founder, Peregrine Ministries International

Fulfilled Through Fear

Find Your True Self and Experience Overwhelming Fulfillment
by Fearing the Infinite, Loving, Dangerous God

Dean C. Halverson

WIPF & STOCK · Eugene, Oregon

FULFILLED THROUGH FEAR
Find Your True Self and Experience Overwhelming Fulfillment by Fearing the Infinite, Loving, Dangerous God

Copyright © 2025 Dean C. Halverson. All rights reserved. Except for brief quotations in critical publications or reviews, no part of this book may be reproduced in any manner without prior written permission from the publisher. Write: Permissions, Wipf and Stock Publishers, 199 W. 8th Ave., Suite 3, Eugene, OR 97401.

Wipf & Stock
An Imprint of Wipf and Stock Publishers
199 W. 8th Ave., Suite 3
Eugene, OR 97401

www.wipfandstock.com

PAPERBACK ISBN: 979-8-3852-4923-7
HARDCOVER ISBN: 979-8-3852-4924-4
EBOOK ISBN: 979-8-3852-4925-1

VERSION NUMBER 06/12/25

All Scripture quotations, unless otherwise indicated, are taken from the Holy Bible, New International Version®, NIV®. Copyright ©1973, 1978, 1984, 2011 by Biblica, Inc.™ Used by permission of Zondervan. All rights reserved worldwide. www.zondervan.com. The "NIV" and "New International Version" are trademarks registered in the United States Patent and Trademark Office by Biblica, Inc.™

Scripture quotations marked (NLT) are taken from Holy Bible, New Living Translation, copyright © 1996, 2004, 2015 by Tyndale House Foundation. Used by permission of Tyndale House Publishers. All rights reserved.

Some content taken from *A Sea Between Us: A True Story of a Man Who Risked Everything for Family and Freedom* by Yosely Pereira and Bill Ivey. Copyright © 2022. Used by permission of Tyndale House Publishers. All rights reserved.

Some content taken from *Transgender to Transformed: A Story of Transition That Will Truly Set You Free* by Laura Perry Smalts. Copyright © 2019. Used by permission of the Genesis Publishing Group. All rights reserved.

Some content taken from *The Last Sweet Mile: A Journey of Brothers* by Allen Levi ©2015 Used by permission of Rabbit Room Press. All rights reserved.

Some content taken from Keith Halverson's posts on Instagram at keiths.creations. Used by permission.

For my wife, Debbie, whose selfless love gave me
the freedom and the time to write this book,

and

for my friend Darrell, who helped me believe that
I had something worthwhile to write and was a
great encouragement to me as I wrote it.

Contents

Introduction | ix

Part I: *Defining* One's True Self

The Shift

Chapter 1: The Shift in Our Culture and in Ourselves | 3

The Options

Chapter 2: We Are Mirrors with Wills | 14

Chapter 3: Defining One's True Self: A Freedom or a Burden? | 29

Part II: *Discovering* One's True Self

Fearing God: What It Means and What It Looks Like

Chapter 4: Utter Dependence: Being Overwhelmed by Our Creator | 47

Chapter 5: Undivided Attention: Come Alive by Focusing on God | 59

Chapter 6: Unshakable Trust: Trusting in the Goodness of
    the God Who Cares | 74

Evidence and Arguments for the God Who Is to Be Feared

Chapter 7: Why Is There Something Rather than Nothing? | 89

CONTENTS

The Blessings of Fearing God

Chapter 8: Seeing God: God Will Dwell with Us | 104

Chapter 9: Fearing God: Bringing Healing to Our Fractured Culture | 122

Our Responses

Chapter 10: Of What Should We Be Most Afraid? | 141

Chapter 11: The God to Be Feared Calls Us to Himself | 146

Chapter 12: Finding Contentment by Fearing God | 155

Concluding Thoughts

Chapter 13: Utter Dependence Is the Foundation for Fearing God | 168

Bibliography | 173

Introduction

CONGRATULATIONS! I COMMEND YOU for reading past the title of this book. When you saw the words "fear" and "fearing" in the title, you probably thought it meant that we are to be afraid of God, right? While we will deal with that matter in chapter 10 (Of What Should We Be Most Afraid?), being afraid of God is not how I understand the way the Bible defines fearing God. While I will spend a larger portion of this book elaborating on what the Bible means by fearing God, let me give a brief illustration up front as to what it means to fear God.

Our son Jonathan attended the Colorado School of Mines in Golden, Colorado. Behind the university is Lookout Mountain where he often rode his mountain bike down a dirt trail as fast as he could. He told me that unless he experienced at least one "Whoa!" moment during a ride, he considered it to be a disappointment. What he meant by a "Whoa!" moment was being on the verge of losing control. Why did he do this? Because that moment of danger grabbed his attention and caused him to feel most alive.

That's a good illustration of what fearing God is all about. We will come most alive and be most fulfilled when our attention is taken off ourselves and focused instead on the infinite God outside us. That's what the fear of God does. It grabs our attention and focuses it on God. Fearing God means living with an overwhelming passion for the overwhelming one and only God.

My hope is to persuade you that you will find your greatest fulfillment by fearing God. Why? Because fearing God is what we were made

INTRODUCTION

for. It flows from who we are, our true self, which is having been made in the image of God. Fearing God is our core purpose in life. It is what will bring us the most fulfillment.

Even if you have doubts about God's existence, I invite you to consider how fearing the God of the Bible gives a better foundation for who you are in all your fullness than any other belief system.

How I Came upon the Topic of Fearing God

Let me tell you how I landed on the topic of fearing God. In 1987 I was experiencing one of the lowest periods of my life. The reason was that for six years my job was to read articles and books that required me to keep up my spiritual defenses. The amount of emotional and intellectual energy expended caused me to become spiritually dry and emotionally depleted. I felt the way Rocky Balboa looked in Rocky III after being knocked out by Clubber Lang in the second round—left eye swollen shut, bleeding from multiple cuts over the face. I needed to be spiritually renewed, refreshed, and revived. I decided to read something I could trust, something that didn't require that I keep up my spiritual defenses. For me, that was the Bible. I wanted to focus especially on those passages that had to do with God. I wanted to think about God alone. As I was reading through the Bible, I came across these words uttered by Moses, the leader of the Israelites. He made the following plea—almost a demand—to God, "Now show me your glory" (Exodus 33:18). As I read those words, my heart was filled with hope. That's exactly what I needed. I needed to see God's glory, to feel his presence. I, like Moses, was crying out to God, "Now show me Your glory!" I needed to know that God was present and that he cared about me as I journeyed through a spiritual wilderness.

I was shocked, though, by God's response to Moses: "No one can see my face, for no one may see me and live" (Exodus 33:20). Why would God say such a thing? Why would he threaten death to those who saw him? Was I mistaken in my belief that God wanted to be in a relationship with us, and we with him? Here in the book of Exodus, Moses was asking for God's presence, but God seems to push him away. Even though God's response puzzled me, I couldn't get those words out of my mind—"No one can see my face, for no one may see me and live." It's like someone had made a statement that was shocking but, at the same time, so profound that you couldn't stop thinking about it.

INTRODUCTION

After giving those words more thought, I came to realize that the reason Moses could not see God's face was because of the infinite difference between God and him. The difference between God and us is infinitely vast. That passage says nothing about Moses' sin being the reason God said, "No one may see me and live." God was not pushing Moses away. He was merely stating the facts of the matter, the reality of the way things are. God, in all the infinite fullness of his being, is too great for us to withstand. The reason we cannot see God has to do with the unimaginable difference between our finite nature and God's infinite nature. We, as finite beings, are not able to withstand the direct, full, and unmediated experience of God's infinite nature. The apostle Paul wrote that God "lives in unapproachable light, whom no one has seen or can see" (1 Timothy 6:16). Since God lives in a light that is unapproachable, then to look at God in all his infinite, unlimited, and unfiltered fullness would be like looking directly at the sun without any protection for the eyes. Blindness would be the inevitable result. Just as we can't look directly at the sun without going blind, neither can we approach the fullness of God's "light" (meaning his infinite nature) without disintegrating. That's how different God is from us.

As I kept thinking about that verse, though, I began to realize that it was talking about exactly the kind of God we need. Why? Because only an infinite God who can overwhelm us for an eternity will fill the desire for eternity that he himself has placed in our hearts. The Bible says that God has "set eternity in the human heart" (Ecclesiastes 3:11). The God who says, "No one can see my face, for no one may see me and live," is the kind of God who we can know for an eternity but never plumb the infinite depths of who he is. We are eternal beings with a God-sized hole in our hearts, and only a relationship of love with the infinite, eternal, personal God can fill that hole.

As I continued reading through the Bible, I kept coming across the theme of fearing God. That phrase confused me. I wondered what it meant. Does it mean to be afraid of God? Does it mean to have a heightened respect or reverence for or awe of God? Why should we fear God? Is it related to the verse that says, "No one can see my face, for no one may see me and live"? If so, how?

I would come across verses such as the following that intrigued me: "Serve the Lord with fear and rejoice with trembling" (Psalm 2:11). How is it possible to rejoice and tremble at the same time? How can someone jump

INTRODUCTION

up and down with joy while also shake in their boots? How are rejoicing and trembling related to fearing the Lord?

Eventually I began to see that fearing God is at the core of who we are. God made us to fear him. Fearing God is our primary purpose in life. The reason I say that is because fearing God means being overwhelmed by who he is in all his infinite fullness. In the coming chapters, I hope to help you understand why fearing God is the most fulfilling thing we can do.

Who This Book Is For

This book is for you who are looking for fulfillment but have been disappointed by the lack of answers that following one's heart gives. It's for you who have attempted to choose your identity but are not sure if you've made the right choice. In fact, having to choose one's own identity has become more like a burden than a freedom. This book is for you who are experiencing anxiety because you had thought you had found your true self, but that discovery has not provided the inner peace you were hoping for. It's for you who are asking what's wrong with us, and are wondering what is the satisfying solution to our problem. It's for those who have a yearning for eternity but don't know how to fulfill that yearning.

This book is not only for you who are searching for answers but also for you who are not searching. You are absolutely certain that you know who you are. You don't have any anxiety about it; you are completely fulfilled in who you are. You know beyond a shadow of a doubt that you are part of a divine oneness that can be characterized as the ultimate in love. I invite you to read further.

This book is even for you who believe that God does not exist and that we are just matter.

This book is also for you who were intrigued by the title *Fulfilled Through Fear*. How can fear be fulfilling? And then you learned through the subtitle—*Find Your True Self and Experience Overwhelming Fulfillment by Fearing the Infinite, Loving, Dangerous God*—that I'm talking about fearing a loving but dangerous God, and that idea raised more questions. Why is God dangerous? Is there value in God being dangerous? How can a dangerous God also be loving? Even more, how can fearing God possibly be fulfilling?

In the end, this book is about finding not just fulfillment but overwhelming fulfillment. And the reason such fulfillment can be overwhelming is because its source is grounded in a God who is overwhelming. That's what fearing an infinite, loving, dangerous God does. It overwhelms us. Fear grabs our attention and causes us to focus on the overwhelming God who is the answer to all our questions, the foundation for all that we are on every level of our being, and the one who satisfies all our yearnings. I will attempt to make the case that we were made to fear God, that it is our primary purpose in life, and that apart from being fulfilled by fearing God, we are settling for less in ourselves.

This book is also for followers of Christ. The concept of fearing God can be easily misunderstood. I have attempted to bring clarity to what the Bible means when it says we are to fear God. I define what the Bible means when it says we are to fear God, and I talk about what are the three characteristics of the person who fears God.

This book is divided into two parts. Part 1 is titled "*Defining* One's True Self." In these chapters I talk about the shift that has taken place in our culture from finding one's identity and meaning in the transcendent God to finding those things by going within and following one's heart. *We* have become the ones who define who we are and what our meaning is. I talk about the problems that can arise from such beliefs.

Part 2 is titled "*Discovering* One's True Self." The word "discovering" is important. It means that we discover the identity and meaning that God has given to us. We are not the source of our identity and meaning; God is. It is in this part of the book that I talk about what it means to fear God. If you are reading this book mostly because you're interested in what the Bible has to say about fearing God, then I invite you to go directly to part 2 (*Discovering* One's True Self).

Theology Can Be Confusing

Since I'm writing to you who might not be followers of Christ, I don't assume that you are familiar with Christian theology. As a result, I explain my theological terms. The one term that I need to explain now is that of the Trinity.

For you who are not familiar with Christian theology, the doctrine of the Trinity might be confusing. Let me clarify the doctrine of the Trinity as much as I can now so that you won't be quite as confused when I talk about it throughout this book. Christians believe, and the Bible teaches, that there is only one God and that God consists of a compound unity, which is described in the doctrine of the Trinity. The doctrine of the Trinity says that God is one in essence and three in persons, where a "person" is a being, whether infinite or finite, uncreated or created, who possesses personal attributes such as emotions, an intellect, and a will and is able to participate in interpersonal relationships with other persons. That way of stating the doctrine means that it does not break the law of noncontradiction, which says that something cannot be both A and non-A at the same time and in the same respect. Essence and persons are distinct and different ideas. Each person of the Trinity—the Father, the Son, and the Holy Spirit—shares the same essence, which means that they each have the same attributes of self-existence, omniscience, omnipotence, infinity, eternity, and absolute holiness, but they are distinct persons.

Each person of the Trinity had a role to play in redemption or salvation history. The Father out of love for the world sent his Son, Jesus Christ, into the world; Jesus, the Son of God, became incarnate as a man, died on our behalf for our sins, and then rose from the dead; and the Holy Spirit indwells us and applies the transforming, life-giving power of Jesus Christ to we who were dead in our sins. He does that so that we could have eternal life, which is being in a relationship of love with God for eternity. As we place our faith and trust in Christ having paid the price completely on our behalf for our sins, we receive the Holy Spirit into our lives.

I realize that my explanation of the Trinity was woefully brief, but I hope it was helpful by way of introducing you to this difficult doctrine.

May you be blessed as you read about finding overwhelming fulfillment by fearing the infinite, loving, dangerous God!

PART I

Defining One's True Self

MANY BELIEVE THAT THE best way to be fulfilled is by following one's heart. What does that mean? It means that we should trust ourselves and do what feels right even if it goes against the accepted beliefs and practices of the culture. Each person has the freedom, the right, and the power to define for themselves their true self and to express it, and it is expected that the culture should not only affirm their choice but also celebrate it.

We will look at the implications of following one's heart and of defining one's true self. Does such a belief set one free and lead to fulfillment?

The Shift

1

The Shift in Our Culture and in Ourselves

OUR CULTURE IS EXPERIENCING an internal struggle. The issue is where to find answers to our most fundamental questions: Who am I? What is my identity? Where can I find meaning in life? How can I experience fulfillment? The choice is between either going within to find our true selves or by going outside ourselves and focusing on the transcendent God.

Professor Carl Trueman, in his book *The Rise and Triumph of the Modern Self,* describes the history of thought that has brought us to the point where finding our authentic, autonomous selves has become the assumed goal of our journey toward meaning and fulfillment. That history has to do with how we have gone from a "mimetic" understanding of meaning to a "poietic" understanding. Here's how Trueman describes the meaning of those terms: "A mimetic view regards the world as having a given order and a given meaning and thus sees human beings as required to discover that meaning and conform themselves to it. Poiesis, by way of contrast, sees the world as so much raw material out of which meaning and purpose can be created by the individual."[1]

To describe the mimetic view, Trueman used the phrases "given order" and "given meaning." Given by whom? By the transcendent Creator God who stands apart from his creation. Our being fulfilled, according to the mimetic view of reality, comes by our discovering who we are as persons who have been made in the image of a transcendent, personal God. The

1. Trueman, *Rise and Triumph,* 39.

poietic view, on the other hand, sees the world as malleable. We ourselves are the ones who create our own meaning and purpose and who define for ourselves who we are in our true selves. Many contend that by defining our true selves, we will be most fulfilled. Given the two choices, the side that seems to be winning the day is the one that advises that we will find fulfillment by finding our true selves and following our hearts.

In his book *Reenchanting Humanity*, Owen Strachan wrote that "the major issue of our time is *anthropology*. Does the human person live in an ordered cosmos and have an appointed identity, or does he make his own identity in a world without God?"[2] The latter view is the one that is most popular in today's culture.

Culture observer and pollster George Barna and his research team noted this movement toward the importance and centrality of the self among the millennials. They defined millennials as those "born from 1984 through 2002," and estimated that there are seventy-eight million of them, "the most populous generation in American society."[3] Barna's survey revealed that millennials place "an excessive emphasis on self" and that their self-image is "built upon self-centeredness, self-reliance, and independence."[4] Such an emphasis on the self grows naturally out of the fact that they are uncertain about God's existence. The study states the following: "The fastest-growing God-view comprises a segment we have labeled the Don'ts. These are people who don't know if God exists; don't care if God exists; or don't believe that God exists. More than four out of 10 Millennials (41 percent) fit this category."[5]

Theologian Thaddeus Williams wrote, "Eighty-six percent [of Americans] believe that to be fulfilled requires you to 'pursue the things you desire most.' Ninety-one percent affirm that 'the best way to find yourself is by looking within yourself.' Such self-centeredness is well on its way to achieving world religion status.... One could make a case that self-worship is the world's fastest growing religion."[6]

If it's true that there is no transcendent God in whose image we are made and who therefore defines us, then it stands to reason that we

---

2. Strachan, *Reenchanting Humanity*, introduction; emphasis in original.
3. Barna, *New Insights*, 5.
4. Barna, *New Insights*, 61, 69.
5. Barna, *New Insights*, 41.
6. Williams, *Don't Follow Your Heart*, introduction.

ourselves would have the ability to define who we are in our true selves, to determine what is our core identity.

In 1992 Justice Anthony Kennedy not only reflected our culture's move to poiesis but even made defining ourselves the law of the land when he wrote the majority opinion in the abortion case titled *Planned Parenthood of Southeastern Pennsylvania v. Casey* (1992): "At the heart of liberty is the right to define one's own concept of existence, of meaning, of the universe, and of the mystery of human life."[7] Kennedy was declaring that the freedom to define ourselves is the essence of liberty. His language in the court decision reflects the belief that we not only have the freedom to create our own identities but that we also have the *right* to do so, putting that freedom on the same level as the freedom of speech, of religion, and of the press.

Sometimes editorial cartoons hit the mark. My local newspaper—*The Gazette* of Colorado Springs—published a cartoon that depicted how the self has become central to how we make moral decisions. Michael Ramirez, the creator of the cartoon, pictured an old-style compass with the markings of north, west, and east on its face. In the place of south, though, the word "SELF" appeared, and the pointer was pointing to that word. The title of the cartoon was "Our Moral Compass."[8] The cartoon was saying that when it comes to our moral compass, the self has become all-important.

My Brother's Experience with the Cultural Shift

The shift from mimesis to poiesis is personal for me because I have a brother who has gone in that direction. I grew up in rural Minnesota with my brother named Keith who is five years older than me. Our parents were strong Christians, and both Keith and I were deeply influenced by their faith as we lived and grew up in their home. After leaving home, though, Keith rejected his Christian faith and joined a spiritually focused group led by a lady who had gone to India, experienced spiritual enlightenment, and then returned to the States to guide others on the path to enlightenment that she had already traveled.

Keith retired from his banking job a few years ago and now spends a large portion of his time doing what he enjoys most, which is writing poetry that expresses his spiritual beliefs. Our niece Maggie finds attractive

---

7. Trueman, *Strange New World*, ch. 8.
8. Ramirez, "Our Moral Compass."

pictures that match perfectly the theme of each poem. She then posts them on Instagram under the account titled "keiths.creations."

According to Keith, ultimate reality, or that which is the ultimate source of all things, is a divine oneness of being, and we are all part of that oneness. We are like streams that flow from the source of divine "Being." That reality, which Keith characterizes as love, is the only true reality. When we see ourselves as separate from that reality of love, we have created our own illusory reality, and our problems of disharmony, division, and hate flow from that illusion of being separated from the inherent oneness of love. Keith wrote the following poem as an expression of that view,

> My heart does burst with blessings,
> my life flows from above,
> for I do know
> within my soul,
> this world is naught but love.[9]

Because only love is real and because divine love flows into our souls and hearts, our greatest purpose in life is to follow the guiding voice that flows from our hearts:

> I am my own religion,
> I cannot other be,
> when in my heart
> and in my soul
> I am the truth of me.[10]

> I shall rise today
> to walk in my own way,
> and listen first
> to my own heart
> and what it has to say.[11]

---

9. Halverson, "My heart does burst."
10. Halverson, "I am my own religion."
11. Halverson, "I shall rise today."

There is no higher purpose,
there is no other choice
than just to listen
to your heart
and follow in its voice.[12]

With such a positive view of humanity, it's not surprising that thousands of people follow Keith on Instagram and are uplifted by his thoughts. He reflects the spiritual beliefs of many in our culture.

Expressive Individualism

In his book *A Secular Age*, philosopher Charles Taylor chronicled the shift that has taken place in our culture.[13] Jonathan Parnell has condensed and simplified the complex arguments contained in Taylor's book, and also outlined the historical flow that has brought us to the predominance of a viewpoint called "expressive individualism." He said that we have gone from "exclusive humanism," which means that there is no transcendent God and that we are therefore on our own, to the "immanent frame," meaning that because there is no God who serves as the foundation for our meaning and identity, we are forced to find those things in that which is "*here*, accessible, [and] earthly." Parnell writes, "If exclusive humanism (i.e., a world without God) leads to the immanent frame (i.e., searching for meaning in the immanent, where we do have contact), then the burden for finding [our] meaning falls on the individual, which is what our society means when you hear talk of 'finding your own way,' or 'doing your own thing,' or 'you do you.' This is expressive individualism."[14] Humanity has pushed God away and has declared that we are ourselves responsible for directing human history. We are on our own. Because meaning, identity, and morals are determined by us alone, we then have the freedom to both find and to express our uniqueness as individuals.

---

12. Halverson, "There is no higher purpose."
13. Taylor, *Secular Age*.
14. Parnell, "Church Discipline."

PART I: *DEFINING ONE'S TRUE SELF*

Shifting from God to Self in a Single Article

I read an article that, surprisingly, made the shift from the transcendent (mimesis) to the immanent (poiesis) within the course of the article itself. That shift was not what I had expected. The article was titled "The Thing in Itself: C. S. Lewis on What We Long for in Our Existential Longing" by Maria Popova. I wanted to read the article because Popova was writing about one of my favorite books (*The Weight of Glory*) by one of my favorite authors (C. S. Lewis) and citing a quote from Lewis that I liked:

> The books or the music in which we thought the beauty was located will betray us if we trust to them; it was not *in* them, it only came *through* them, and what came through them was longing. These things—the beauty, the memory of our own past—are good images of what we really desire; but if they are mistaken for the thing itself they turn into dumb idols, breaking the hearts of their worshipers. For they are not the thing itself; they are only the scent of a flower we have not found, the echo of a tune we have not heard, news from a country we have never visited.[15]

I like that quote because it speaks of how the reality in which we live will not fulfill our longing because it is not "the thing itself." The beauty in our present reality serves a vital purpose, though, which is to point to the one who created that beauty. He is the "thing itself," and only he is enough to fulfill the deep longing within our hearts. We should not settle for merely "the scent of a flower" or the "echo of a tune." Doing so would be like my being satisfied with only letters from my wife but not longing for the very presence of my wife.

I read Popova's article thinking she would affirm Lewis's premise. I was jolted out of that thinking, though, when I read her conclusion:

> For Lewis, who was religious, this notion of "the thing in itself"— the ultimate object of longing—was anchored in his understanding of God. For me, it calls to mind Virginia Woolf's exquisite epiphany about the meaning of art and life, found while strolling through her flower-garden: "Behind the cotton wool is hidden a pattern . . . the whole world is a work of art . . . there is no Shakespeare . . . no Beethoven . . . no God; we are the words; we are the music; we are the thing itself."[16]

---

15. Lewis, *Weight of Glory*, 4–5.
16. Popova, "Thing in Itself."

THE SHIFT IN OUR CULTURE AND IN OURSELVES

As I read her conclusion, I wondered if I had read it correctly. Did Popova realize that her final statement, in which she affirms her agreement with Woolf's statement that "we are the thing itself," contradicts Lewis's premise that God is the "thing itself"? Did she realize that the two perspectives are mutually exclusive, that they cannot be reconciled with each other, and that both cannot be true? Did she think that she was merely sharing two perspectives that, while they differed from each other, were in essential agreement because they both talked about "the thing itself"?

What Popova didn't seem to realize was that Lewis's "religious" perspective is not merely "his understanding of God," but that he was making a claim about truth that is objective and absolute. He was not merely stating one relative perspective among many, but he was making an exclusive claim to truth that spoke about how we should understand the nature of reality.

Lewis's belief that there is a transcendent God who created all things cannot be reconciled with Woolf's statement that "there is . . . no God." Our being "the thing itself" and God being "the thing itself" cannot both be true. Consider, again, the statement by Virginia Woolf that inspired Popova: "The whole world is a work of art . . . there is no Shakespeare . . . no Beethoven . . . no God; we are the words; we are the music; we are the thing itself." What she's saying is that art does not need an artist, that the plays of Shakespeare did not need an author, and that the symphonies of Beethoven did not need a composer. She's saying that, since Shakespeare and Beethoven were part of the beauty of the world as a work of art, they were merely reflecting their own beautiful nature when they created the art that they did. In the same way, "the whole world" as a work of art does not need a Creator, an ultimate Artist. Why not? Because the world as a work of art is reflecting the beauty that is inherent in it, not the beauty of some Creator that is separate from and transcendent to it. Such a thought, Popova was saying, was merely Lewis's understanding of God and his supposedly relative religious perspective. We know now though, claims Popova, that "we are the thing itself," that we in our true selves are the source of beauty and art. To experience our true selves is to experience the very source of the beauty and value that is within us, not transcendent to us.

Popova reflects the shift that has taken place in our culture and in ourselves. The transcendent has morphed into the immanent. The "thing itself" has moved from the being of God to our own being. Today, many believe that we will come alive and be fulfilled not when we are in a relationship with the transcendent, personal God but when we have the freedom to define our own identity, our own meaning, and to follow our hearts.

Many of us feel entirely satisfied with Popova's idea that we are the "thing itself," that we are ourselves the source of creativity and beauty that is seen in reality. We don't see a need to invoke a transcendent Creator God to explain beauty and meaning. We are enough in ourselves.

Are we indeed, though, enough in ourselves? I want us to consider that we are not enough in ourselves. Why would I say that? Because we can't be enough in ourselves. In ourselves alone, we can't explain even our own existence. How did we come to exist? Did we bring ourselves into existence? No! So, then, we are not enough in ourselves. We need something outside us to explain our existence.

Why do we have value as persons? Is our value as persons based on something intrinsic to us? Is it enough to say that I have value as a person simply because I exist? Cockroaches also exist. But you would squash one with your foot if it invaded your home, would you not? What makes you more valuable than a cockroach? There has to be something more than mere existence that serves as the foundation for our value as persons. Is it consciousness? Is it complexity? Is it rationality? Are those qualities enough to provide a foundation for our value as persons? Who determines whether we have value or not? The government? What if the government decides that the class of people to which you belong does not have value? Are you willing to settle for that? To what would you point by way of objecting to the government that denies your value as a person? The point is that there has to be something outside us that we would point to as the foundation for our value, and that means that we are not enough in ourselves.

The Kind of Foundation Needed

The God who has personal attributes and who has made us in his image gives us the metaphysical foundation that is necessary to uphold every aspect of who we are as persons—our value as persons, our morals, our intelligence, our wills, and our purpose.

On July 4, 1776, the Founding Fathers of the United States of America ratified the Declaration of Independence, which in part stated, "We hold these truths to be self-evident, that all men are created equal, that they are endowed by their Creator with certain unalienable Rights, that among these are Life, Liberty and the pursuit of Happiness."[17] Then, on December 10, 1948, almost two centuries later, the General Assembly of the United Nations stated the following in the first line of the preamble of their Universal Declaration for Human Rights: "Whereas recognition of the inherent dignity and of the equal and inalienable rights of all members of the human family is the foundation of freedom, justice and peace in the world . . ." What these two declarations share is the belief that every person has human rights that can't be separated from them because they have dignity and worth that is inherent to them.

Their differences, however, are significant and fundamental. Whereas the Declaration of Independence lays the foundation for our equality and worth as persons in the fact that we were each made by a common Creator, the Universal Declaration for Human Rights gives no such transcendent foundation. It says, instead, that it is the "recognition of the inherent dignity and of the equal and inalienable rights of all members of the human family" that is the foundation for those rights. They have replaced the transcendent Creator God as the foundation for our rights with merely our recognition of those rights, which is nothing but the self. Perhaps they worded their declaration the way they did to be diplomatic, but still, it's like saying that we all agree that we have rights as individuals but refuse to acknowledge the necessity for having a metaphysical foundation for those rights. What if someone disagrees by saying that a particular segment of society is not entitled to human rights? Then to what do we point as the foundation for those rights? We would have nothing to point to beyond our mere assertion that we all have rights.

Consider another example of how we need a transcendent foundation for our rights and value as persons. When defending his action of breaking the laws that segregated Black people from white, Dr. Martin Luther King Jr., the great social reformer and civil rights leader, wrote, "How does one determine when a law is just or unjust? A just law is a man-made code that squares with the moral law or the law of God. An unjust law is a code that is out of harmony with the moral law."[18] Dr. King was saying that there is a moral realm that stands outside the realm of man-made laws and that serves as a foundation for the just nature of our man-made laws. If our man-made laws do not conform to that transcendent moral law, then it is unjust. Again, though, this example points to how our laws need

---

17. Declaration of Independence, para. 2.
18. King, *Testament of Hope*, 293.

a moral foundation, and the only adequate foundation for our morality is a morally holy and personal God.

Summary

Our culture has gone through a major shift. Whereas we used to locate the source of our meaning and identity in a transcendent God, we now look inside ourselves for those things. The question, though, is whether such an immanent foundation is enough to uphold our meaning, identity, morality, and our value as persons.

Questions for Personal Reflection or Group Discussion

1. What is the shift that our culture has gone through?
2. Do you agree that we are not enough in ourselves? Why or why not?
3. In what do you locate the foundation for your meaning and identity? In yourself or in something outside yourself?
4. If someone were to deny that you have value as a person, to what would you point as the foundation for your value as a person?

The Options

2

We Are Mirrors with Wills

WITH ALL DUE RESPECT, Maria Popova was wrong. We are not the "thing in itself." God is. We did not create ourselves; God created us, and he created us in his image: "God created man in his own image, in the image of God he created him; male and female he created them" (Genesis 1:27). A piece of art does need an artist. God is the Artist, and we are his work of art. Just as it is the role of a piece of art to reflect the creativity, skill, and inspiration of the artist, so too is it our role as beings made in God's image to reflect the nature and personality of God, the ultimate Artist.

Theologian Anthony Hoekema wrote in his book *Created in God's Image*, "As a mirror reflects, so man should reflect God. When one looks at a human being, one ought to see in him or her a certain reflection of God."[1] As persons made in God's image, our role—our very purpose in life—is to reflect that image. Our purpose, as God's work of art, is to reflect the image of the Artist who created us. Reflecting God's image is who we were intended to be; it's our primary purpose in life. We will not find fulfillment and come alive until we reflect God's image. Owen Strachan wrote the following in his book *Reenchanting Humanity*:

> We are not the end . . . ; it is God who is the purpose of all things. We exist for his glory. We "receive" and "return" his glory through knowing and adoring our Maker and Redeemer. We live only by his allowance, and we love him only by his decree. So far from being a project of self-expression and internalized meaning, life

---

1. Hoekema, *Created in God's Image*, 67.

is one grand affair of the godly kind. It is all from God, in God, and to God. It is not self-discovery we seek; it is God-exaltation that we crave. In such an existence, we not only find the deepest happiness there is, but . . . we find who we are and what we were intended to be.[2]

As Strachan has written, our role as beings made in the image of God is to exalt God. That is where we find our "deepest happiness." It is "who we are and who we were intended to be."

I agree with Hoekema's statement that we were made to mirror God's image. When you're talking about persons reflecting God rather than an inanimate mirror, though, the situation is not as simple as a mirror automatically reflecting whatever is in front of it. The mirror doesn't have a choice about reflecting that image. When it comes to we as persons acting as mirrors to reflect God's image, though, it gets more complicated. Why? Because persons have wills and, therefore, the ability to make choices. That's part of what it means to be a person. While the blueprint of our having been made in the image of God is permanent and unchangeable, we must nevertheless choose to reflect that blueprint, which is the image of God.

We have a problem, though, and that is that we have chosen to reflect the creation rather than the Creator. How have we done that? By choosing to glorify ourselves rather than glorifying God by reflecting him. We glorify ourselves by making ourselves more important than the Creator God.

The point that I'm making is that we have two choices. The first choice has to do with the nature of the ultimate reality—God—we choose to reflect. Do we believe that ultimate reality is personal or impersonal, material or spiritual? The second choice has to do with whether we will choose to glorify God by reflecting him or to glorify ourselves by reflecting ourselves. The first choice has to do with the nature of the God we choose to reflect, and the second choice has to do with whether we choose to reflect God or ourselves.

Reflecting *the Image of God*

In the following section we will look at three examples of belief systems that fail to supply a sufficient foundation for who we are as persons. In fact, they even remove the foundation for our existence and value as persons altogether. Because they deny the existence of a personal, transcendent

2. Strachan, *Reenchanting Humanity*, ch. 1.

Creator God, they remove the only foundation that is adequate to uphold who we are as persons. We will be looking at three examples, two of which come from the idea that ultimate reality is an impersonal oneness of spirit, and the third example comes from the idea that ultimate reality is an impersonal oneness of matter.

Why am I doing this? Why am I going through the exercise of looking at examples of teachings where their view of ultimate reality is anything but the personal, transcendent Creator God of the Bible? I'm not doing it because I have anything personally against these authors. I'm not attacking them as persons. I am, however, bringing their belief systems into question. I'm doing this for two reasons.

First, their belief systems are usually the ones that are behind the belief that we can find our true selves and must follow our hearts. If there is no transcendent God in whose image we are made, then it is up to us to define for ourselves who we are in our true selves and to follow our hearts. If ultimate reality is a oneness that is more like a force than a person, then we as persons do indeed have the freedom to declare who we are in our true selves.

Second, I'm looking at their belief systems critically because I want us to see the effects that denying the transcendent, personal God has on our personhood. Even more, if we believe in a concept of ultimate reality (or God) that is not sufficient as a foundation to uphold all of who we are as persons, then we should be honest enough with ourselves to realize that our belief system might be wrong and that we are worshiping the wrong god.

This all comes back to the basic meaning of fearing God, which is to acknowledge that the God who created us is the only one who is worthy of being feared and worshiped. We were made to reflect the personal Creator God of the Bible who made us in his image. That image is our true selves, our deepest identity.

Trying to Mix Oil and Water

What is often the case with those who teach that ultimate reality is an impersonal divine oneness is that they mix the language of the impersonal with that of the personal. For example, they will say that an *impersonal* force exhibits *personal* characteristics such as intelligence or love. The two languages—the personal and impersonal—can't be mixed, however, because they contradict each other. They have mutually exclusive characteristics.

An impersonal oneness does not have the ability to be conscious, to have intelligence, or to think. An impersonal oneness is not able to love because love is inherently interpersonal. It's impossible to have a personal relationship with the water in a glass. The water cannot relate to you as a person. Such an impossible scenario, though, is exactly what mixing the language of the personal with the impersonal does. It mixes what cannot be mixed. The purpose for doing so is to make God less scary, less other, and less fearful. In the process of making God less scary, less other, and less fearful, though, they make him into a one-dimensional god who has no depth.

Dr. Deepak Chopra, famed writer on healing and spiritual matters, is an example of one who mixes the language of the impersonal with that of the personal when talking about the nature of ultimate reality. We will see that happening in the following quote from Chopra. The context of this quote is the event of his father's death:

> I am questioning the whole idea that there is such a thing as a person.
>
> In India, death is much more dramatic: I'm cremating him [Chopra's father] and 300 yards away there are kids flying a kite, using the draft of the cremation fire to fly the kite. And you know, in a few hours the person has totally disappeared. You collect the bones; they're like little pieces of ivory. You wash them in the Ganges, and then the person merges back into the energy and intelligence of the universe from where he came.
>
> So you start to wonder: for all eternity, we are there in that primordial quantum soup. And for a few years, which is nothing—it's like the flicker of a firefly in the middle of the night—we are individuals. And so we identify with the flicker instead of the real home that we have. And if we did identify with that real home, I think we would have a lot more love and compassion . . . because we would recognize our oneness, our inseparability. We would recognize that there's nothing other than that big ecosystem, that primordial soup from which we come and to which we go. You're not independent of it.[3]

We see how Chopra mixes the language of the impersonal with that of the personal when he characterizes ultimate reality as "the energy and intelligence of the universe" and as "the primordial quantum soup." "Energy" and the "primordial quantum soup" are impersonal, but "intelligence" is personal. Ultimate reality cannot be both impersonal and

3. Scheinin, "Father's death sends," 1.

personal at the same time. A "primordial quantum soup" is not able to act in a way that demonstrates intelligence because it is incapable of doing those things that an intelligent being would do, such as learn, think, have relationships, and make choices. The same could be said of the "energy" that Chopra speaks of.

Chopra also calls the "primordial quantum soup" our "real home." By using the term "home," he's raising the feelings of love and acceptance that we normally connect with the idea of home. The feelings of home are usually associated with loving relationships. At the same time, though, he's using the idea of the "primordial quantum soup" to question "the whole idea that there is such a thing as a person." Which is it? Is the primordial soup a place where there is warmth and love between persons at home, or is it a cold force that absorbs all persons into itself? Again, he's mixing the personal with the impersonal. It's impossible, however, to mix them. An impersonal force can't exhibit personal attributes. Ultimate reality is either personal or impersonal, but not both.

Chopra surmises, moreover, that we would have "a lot more love and compassion" for each other if we recognized "our oneness, our inseparability" in the "primordial soup." Is that true? Consider, for example, the fact that our bodies consist of 60 percent water. Does the knowledge that you and your neighbor are each connected in your essence to the impersonal essence of the ocean cause you to love him more? When you see your neighbor, do you think to yourself, "I really should treat him better because both our bodies consist of 60 percent water"? Probably not.

The result of Chopra's worldview where he mixes the personal with the impersonal is that he makes God into a one-dimensional being whose only acceptable response to humanity is a one-dimensional love that lacks depth, passion, and justice. Does not a God who truly loves have the right to be morally outraged when he sees humans hurting, hating, demeaning, and killing each other? Does not the God who truly loves have the right to judge us for actions that go against his holy character? Love demands justice. Christian thinker and writer Drew Dyck writes, "To fear the Lord is not to suggest God is callous or cruel. Just the opposite, in fact. It is God's consuming love that makes him so dangerous. Because he cares deeply for his creation, he will not tolerate evil and injustice forever. Sin corrupts and destroys what he has created. So when he sees that happening, he is incensed and becomes very dangerous indeed."[4] Chopra's one-dimensional

4. Dyck, *Yawning at Tigers*, 60.

god, however, is incapable of providing that kind of justice and that kind of passion for the well-being of humanity.

We're uncomfortable, though, with a personal God who is absolutely holy and good. So, in order to make God more safe, more comfortable, and more understandable, we make God into a one-dimensional being whose only acceptable emotion is that of love. By doing so, his love also becomes one-dimensional. If we as human beings have value, though, then God's love must also include such seemingly distasteful emotions as wrath, righteous anger, and the desire for justice. Biblically speaking, those distasteful emotions flow out of God's love; they are not contrary to God's love. How, after all, do we think God should view the drug dealers who lace their pills with fentanyl and as a result cause thousands of young lives to be snuffed out? What should God do with that? Should he look on such actions with acceptance and affirmation? What about the husband and father who, out of lust, leaves the family, marries another woman, and destroys the lives of his wife and family? How should God view that? What about the human traffickers who, out of greed, ruin the lives of young girls? What does the God who is love do with that? Were not those young girls made in his image? Did they not have value as persons? If God does not react to such evil with righteous anger, wrath, and a concern for justice, then none of us has value as persons and there is no foundation for justice.

To make God completely safe, though, we go beyond making him merely one-dimensional to making him impersonal. When God becomes the impersonal source of being that underlies all that exists, then the only requirement for being connected to him is to exist. When the only requirement to be loved by God is to exist, then the meaning of love is diminished to nothing more than us as individuals being like a drop of water that is absorbed into the vast oneness of the ocean. That end, though, is eternal death, not eternal life, because it means the elimination of the person in the impersonal oneness.

Also, Chopra's concept of ultimate reality being an impersonal spiritual force removes our ability to be in an interpersonal relationship with God. He's promoting the illusion that as we merge into the primordial soup, which he calls "home," we will experience only love. He fails to recognize, though, that when we as persons merge into that primordial soup, we lose our personhood, and as a result, there is no person to love or to be loved. Neither is there a personal God who can love us or who can serve as a foundation for our existence as persons and for our true selves. Chopra is maintaining the myth that we as persons have arisen out of the impersonal primordial soup, which means he believes an effect can be greater than its cause.

Chopra espouses an idea about ultimate reality that claims to be able to mix the personal with the impersonal, but in the process, the personal has become lost in the impersonal. Chopra's teachings cannot uphold the nature of all that we are as persons, and as a result, we cannot find the foundation for our true selves in them.

Merging into the Undifferentiated Divine Oneness

Eckhart Tolle, in his book *The Power of Now*, presents an example of what happens to our personhood when ultimate reality is seen as an impersonal oneness. Tolle writes about how our true self is connected to and one with the ultimate being:

> The word enlightenment conjures up the idea of some super-human accomplishment, and the ego likes to keep it that way, but it is simply your natural state of *felt* oneness with Being. It is a state of connectedness with something immeasurable and indestructible, something that, almost paradoxically, is essentially you and yet is much greater than you. It is finding your true nature beyond name and form. The inability to feel this connectedness gives rise to the illusion of separation from yourself and from the world around you. . . .
>
> Being is the eternal, ever-present One Life beyond the myriad forms of life that are subject to birth and death. However, Being is not only beyond but also deep within every form as its innermost invisible and indestructible essence. This means that it is accessible to you now as your own deepest self, your true nature.[5]

How could one not feel good about oneself after reading that? Tolle is telling us that we are connected to the oneness of being, which is immeasurable and indestructible, which means that in our essence we, too, are immeasurable and indestructible. That is our "deepest self," our "true nature." We could not feel more affirmed in who we are.

A problem arises, though, when Tolle fleshes out the implications of that divine connection: "Having access to that formless realm is truly liberating. It frees you from bondage to form and identification with form. It is

---

5. Tolle, *Power of Now*, 12–13; emphasis in original.

life in its undifferentiated state prior to its fragmentation into multiplicity. We may call it the Unmanifested, the invisible Source of all things, the Being within all beings. It is a realm of deep stillness and peace, but also of joy and intense aliveness."[6] The most significant word in that quote is "undifferentiated." What does it mean to be "undifferentiated"? It means "without distinctions." All distinctions, including distinctions between persons, disappear in the realm of that which is undifferentiated. As Tolle says, the undifferentiated state is "prior to its fragmentation into multiplicity." What is the "multiplicity"? It's us! It's the realm where we exist as persons who are in relationship with each other. Tolle writes that this undifferentiated realm is a "realm of deep stillness and peace, but also of joy and intense aliveness." Who, though, is experiencing this "stillness and peace," this "joy and intense aliveness"? No one. The reality of our personhood has disappeared into the undifferentiated oneness of being. Our reality as persons has merged into the oneness of the great undifferentiation. The unintentional consequence of believing that we are connected to the impersonal divine essence is that we lose the foundation for our existence and value as persons.

Tolle begins by talking about how we are in our essence immeasurable and indestructible because we are connected to that kind of being. That, to Tolle, is the nature of the God we reflect. In the end, though, because this God is an undifferentiated oneness, we lose our personhood altogether, which means that there is no one to experience the joy that Tolle says awaits us. Tolle's view of God being an undifferentiated oneness will not provide an adequate foundation for our true selves, nor will it fulfill us as persons who need love, identity, meaning, and relationships.

Matter Produces the Mind but Eliminates the Person

Dr. Patricia Churchland is our third and final example of a belief system where a view of ultimate reality is not capable of sustaining our existence and value as persons and, therefore, our true selves. Churchland has developed a theory of the brain called neurophilosophy. At the core of that philosophy is what Churchland calls "eliminative materialism" (EM). The term "eliminative" refers to Churchland's desire to eliminate the commonly held belief that the idea of a person includes an immaterial mind. Churchland describes her theory of how the material brain works in this way:

---

6. Tolle, *Power of Now*, 130.

PART I: *DEFINING ONE'S TRUE SELF*

> In order for an organism to see, its nervous system must be affected by the world external to it. . . . Out of that stimulus array, the brain must concoct an interpretation of what in the external world corresponds to the received pattern of light. And of course, there is no one inside to see the array and identify it as the sort of pattern made by, say, a bird or a pineapple. There are just networks of neurons that interact with each other. . . . Since it cannot be magic, there must be mechanisms.[7]

In the above quote, Churchland dismisses the existence of a conscious person—"there is no one inside to see the array"—and replaces it with a "mechanism" consisting of "just networks of neurons that interact with each other." In another part of her work, she describes those neurons as "individually blind and individually stupid."[8] If the brain works like a mechanism without a conscious mind to guide it, then how does the physical brain "recognize" external objects? Churchland theorizes that it does so by the brain matching the incoming image with images that are already stored in the brain. So how does the brain store images? By organizing the properties of each object according to their respective categories: movement, faces, color, shapes, smells, tastes, etc. Then, when we see that image, the brain matches it to images that are already stored.

One of the more baffling implications of Churchland's eliminative materialism theory is that Churchland's physicalism eliminates our ability to have beliefs. How, though, can one hold to the belief that we cannot have beliefs? Even to ask the question reveals the inherent contradiction. After all, is not the belief that we don't have beliefs a belief? How does Churchland get around this contradiction? She does so by saying that "folk psychology is the only theory available *now*."[9] She hopes, however, to change that through her theory of eliminative materialism.

How does Patricia Churchland conclude her book on neurophilosophy? I ask this question because the concluding sentence of any book says a lot about the author's purpose in writing that book. It's usually the culmination of what the author has been trying to say. Churchland concludes her book with this sentence: "So it is that the brain investigates the brain, theorizing about what brains do when they theorize, finding out what brains do

---

7. Churchland, *Neurophilosophy*, 461.
8. Churchland, *Neurophilosophy*, 406.
9. Churchland, *Neurophilosophy*, 397; emphasis in original.

when they find out, and being changed forever by the knowledge."[10] Let me make two observations about that concluding sentence.

First, all reference to anything of a personal nature is gone; the person has been eliminated, which, of course, was the goal of Churchland's *eliminative* materialism. Churchland doesn't say *we* investigate or *scientists* investigate. She instead says that the *brain* is doing the investigating and the theorizing. After having removed the "I" of folk psychology, all that's left in her naturalistic system is the mechanism of the brain investigating, theorizing, finding out, and being changed.

Second, Churchland writes that after the brain has done its investigating and theorizing, it will be "changed forever." What, though, does "changed forever" mean? Changed for what? For the better? What does "better" mean in a mechanistic, matter-only world? More efficient? Perhaps. But how would a material brain that cannot have beliefs know if it's being more efficient? The phrase "changed forever" could not mean morally better since Churchland's physicalist theory has eliminated any nonmaterial realm where morals could exist. Based on the whole purpose of Churchland's neurophilosophy and more specifically on her eliminative materialism theory, and based on her antagonism toward "folk psychology," the reader is left to surmise that what she means by being "changed forever" is that the brain would finally recognize that there is no mind, no person, and no "I" within the brain. There are not even any beliefs.

Churchland begins with matter and ends with matter and actively argues against the existence of a nonmaterial mind that is able to have beliefs. The ultimate reality that she has chosen to reflect is matter and only matter. Her teachings provide no foundation for our existence and value as persons and, subsequently, neither do they provide a foundation for our true selves.

A Foundation for All of Who We Are

My purpose for critically analyzing the teachings of Deepak Chopra, Eckhart Tolle, and Patricia Churchland is not because they have an oversized influence on our culture, but to show what happens when we reject the personal God who made us in his image. We've seen that anything less than a personal, transcendent Creator God is insufficient as a foundation for upholding our existence and our value as persons.

---

10. Churchland, *Neurophilosophy*, 482.

PART I: *DEFINING ONE'S TRUE SELF*

The kind of thinking that we see in Chopra, Tolle, and Churchland has to eventually have an effect on our culture. In fact, George Barna and his research team noticed such an effect on the millennials: "Millennials . . . are twice as likely as older adults to diminish the value of human life by describing human beings as either 'material substance only' [the view represented by Patricia Churchland] or their very existence as 'an illusion' [the view represented by Deepak Chopra and Eckhart Tolle]. . . . Their perspective is simply that people are not inherently valuable creatures; they are neither made in the image of God nor imbued with value due to their creation by God and being loved by Him."[11]

Our view of ultimate reality must serve as an adequate foundation for all of who we are as persons, including our morals; our value as persons; our longing for eternity; our intellect, emotions, and will; and our need for love and relationships. We are like the rooms of a house that require a single foundation to unify and uphold the entire structure. The most adequate explanation and foundation for our existence and value as persons is a personal Creator God who made us in his image.

The story of Dr. Paul Kalanithi is instructive here. At the age of thirty-six, he was diagnosed as having lung cancer. Realizing that he didn't have long to live, he decided to chronicle his journey toward death in *When Breath Becomes Air*. In that book he wrote that even though he "had been raised in a devout Christian family," he "came to believe in the possibility of a material conception of reality, an ultimately scientific worldview that would grant a complete metaphysics, minus outmoded concepts like souls, God, and bearded white men in robes."[12] He had become a thoroughgoing materialist who believed that the scientific method could give a complete view of reality where the immaterial, unseen things such as souls and God were no longer needed. But then he became aware of a problem, which was that the scientific method—based on observability, repeatability, and a material view of reality—eliminates the very intangibles that give meaning to our lives:

> The paradox is that scientific methodology is the product of human hands and thus cannot reach permanent truth. We build scientific theories to organize and manipulate the world, to reduce phenomena into manageable units. Science is based on reproducibility and manufactured objectivity. As strong as that makes its

11. Barna, *New Insights*, 48.
12. Kalanithi, *When Breath Becomes Air*, part 2.

ability to generate claims about matter and energy, it also makes scientific knowledge inapplicable to the existential, visceral nature of human life, which is unique and subjective and unpredictable. Science may provide the most useful way to organize empirical, reproducible data, but its power to do so is predicated on its inability to grasp the most central aspects of human life: hope, fear, love, hate, beauty, envy, honor, weakness, striving, suffering, virtue.[13]

Even though Kalanithi realized that the scientific method failed to account for the "intangibles" of life, which are the things that give life meaning, he still concluded that "between the core passions and scientific theory, there will always be a gap. No system of thought can contain the fullness of human experience."[14] Is that true? Is it true that "no system of thought can contain the fullness of human experience"? No, it's not! If a worldview (what Kalanithi calls "a system of thought") can't explain all of reality, then it is insufficient as a belief system that claims to be true.

One of the ways to test whether a worldview is true is to ask, How well does it explain all of reality? This is called the comprehensive test for truth. Philosopher Douglas Groothuis writes, "A *worldview* has a broad reference range; it attempts to map the rudiments of reality comprehensively. If it gives us no explanation for important aspects of life—matters pertaining to meaning, morality, and mortality—something is amiss, since these questions are perennial and pertinent."[15] Groothuis says that a worldview must be able to explain "meaning, morality, and mortality." Meaning: What is our purpose in life? Morality: Do we have a sufficient foundation for our morals and for our sense of justice? Mortality: What happens after death? Do we have immaterial spirits that continue to exist after the death of the body? These are the some of the intangibles that Kalanithi's secular and materialistic worldview could not explain but that any worldview must be able to explain in order to make the claim to be true. For a belief system to be true, it must have a cause that is able to explain the effects that we see in the world, both material and immaterial.

For example, that cause and effect relationship must be present to explain all that we are as persons. The effects of our personal nature, our values, our morals, and our hopes need a cause that is sufficient. Because we were made in the image of God, who made us to reflect him, the God

---

13. Kalanithi, *When Breath Becomes Air*, part 2.
14. Kalanithi, *When Breath Becomes Air*, part 2.
15. Groothuis, *Christian Apologetics*, 45; emphasis in original.

who created us must have personal characteristics to uphold our existence and value as persons. If we make God less than who he is, such as an impersonal oneness of spirit or matter, then our existence and value as persons are undermined as well. The teachings of Chopra, Tolle, and Churchland are examples of that happening.

Reflecting the Image of God

Now we move from talking about the nature of the God we choose to reflect to talking about the act of reflecting itself. Since we are persons whose purpose is to "mirror," or to reflect, the glory and the image of God, we have a choice not only about the nature of the God we will reflect, which is what we covered in the previous section, but also about whether we will glorify either the Creator or the creation through our reflection. It is an either-or proposition. We reflect either the Creator or the creation, but not both. By "creation," I'm referring primarily to ourselves. We have a choice as to whether we reflect God or ourselves. By saying that we reflect ourselves, I mean that we define our true selves, and then we reflect nothing more than the self we have defined. We reflect nothing but ourselves and nothing beyond ourselves. This is the poiesis model that Carl Trueman talked about where we look to ourselves for our meaning in life. Defining our true selves is what is most important to us. Popular maxims for poieses include "Follow your heart," "To thine own self be true," "Live your truth," and "You are enough."

What happens when we decide to not reflect our Creator but to reflect ourselves instead? We actually become less than ourselves. What is a mirror that reflects nothing but itself? It is less than itself. The whole purpose of a mirror is to reflect the reality outside it. A mirror that reflects only itself fails to live up to the purpose for which it was made. That's also true when we choose to reflect nothing but ourselves. If we reflect only ourselves, we will fail to live up to the purpose for which we were made. When we define ourselves as nothing but ourselves and not as persons made in the image of God, then we become less than who we were intended to be. We lose ourselves when we choose to define ourselves as nothing but ourselves. We can find our true selves only when we realize that we were made in the image of God. He is the foundation for our true self. Anything less than a personal God as our foundation diminishes who we are as persons. We were made to reflect a personal God outside us who made us in his image as persons.

When writing about his own search for his self, author Eric Metaxas raised some interesting questions: "The idea that we can find ourselves is itself fraught with problems, though it's the sort of thing we talk about as though we all understand what it means, but do we? Who are we exactly that we need to be found by ourselves? And which self is finding which other self? Does it make any real sense, or is it simply an empty figure of speech with the barest purchase in reality? Is it really any more meaningful than 'um'?"[16] Metaxas has a point. It makes no sense to define ourselves by ourselves because a definition that includes nothing but itself carries no meaning. It's like saying that the definition of a cow is a cow. No information is being communicated. A definition of the self must include not only something outside it but it must also uphold every part of who we are as persons (emotions, will, intellect, value, morals, love, hope, etc.). That's what being made in the image of a God who has personal attributes does. An ultimate reality that is by nature impersonal will not work as a sufficient foundation for ourselves as persons.

In summary, we are "mirrors with wills," and we have two choices to make. First, we must choose the nature of the God we reflect, whether impersonal or personal. While an impersonal god is safe, it removes the foundation for our value and existence as persons. Only a personal God can serve as a foundation that is able to uphold all of who we are as persons. Second, we must choose to reflect either ourselves or God. When we choose to reflect only ourselves, we become less than ourselves by not living according to the purpose for which we were made, just as a mirror that reflects only itself fails to live up to its purpose. When we choose to reflect the God who made us in his image, though, then we are fulfilled by living according to the purpose for which we were made. As we will see in the next chapter, it is not only more fulfilling but also more freeing when we live according to our God-given purpose and pattern (the image of God within us) than when we fight against it.

Questions for Personal Reflection or Group Discussion

1. What is our purpose in life?
2. Do you agree that a personal Creator God is the best foundation for our existence and value as persons? Why or why not?

---

16. Metaxas, *Fish out of Water*, ch. 32.

PART I: *DEFINING ONE'S TRUE SELF*

3. What is the comprehensive test for truth? How does it help us know what is true?

4. What do you think of the quote from Eric Metaxas?

5. Why is ultimate reality as an impersonal force of either spirit or energy not an adequate foundation for our existence and value as persons?

3

Defining One's True Self: A Freedom or a Burden?

IN THE PREVIOUS CHAPTER we talked about how, as persons made in the image of God, our primary purpose in life is to reflect God. Our culture, though, says that a person's primary purpose is to define one's true self. There is indeed a case to be made for that belief, especially when it comes to our being free. Is there not freedom in defining ourselves? Are we not completely free when we can choose who we want to be? Is it not liberating to define our true selves? As people whose purpose is to reflect ourselves, we have a completely blank canvas on which we can paint anything we want. On the other hand, by saying that I must reflect the God who has made us in his image, am I not then restricted and limited to reflecting a certain image? Which is most fulfilling—to define one's true self or to live according to the image of God that has been given to us?

When You See My Face, You Will Die

There is a fascinating interaction between God and Moses that intrigues me. Moses, the leader of the Israelites, made the following plea to God, "Now show me your glory" (Exodus 33:18). God responded, "You cannot see my face, for no one may see me and live" (Exodus 33:20). Interestingly, though, God was not the only one who said those words to Moses. The Pharaoh of Egypt was the first to do so. Here's the situation.

PART I: *DEFINING ONE'S TRUE SELF*

Moses had approached Pharaoh for permission to take the enslaved people of Israel on a three-day journey out of the city so they could worship their God. Pharaoh refused Moses' request. As a result, God, through Moses, started raining plagues upon Egypt to show Pharaoh who the true God was and to convince Pharaoh to let his people go. After nine devastating plagues (rivers turned to blood, frogs, gnats, flies, death of livestock, boils, hail, locusts, darkness), Pharaoh still stubbornly refused to release Moses and the Hebrew nation to worship their God. Pharaoh told Moses, "Get out of my sight! Make sure you do not appear before me again! The day you see my face you will die" (Exodus 10:28). Sound familiar?

It can't be a coincidence that Moses is confronted with almost the exact same words from two different sources. What is the significance of that? It's that the real confrontation was not between Moses and Pharaoh but between the true God and the false god, between the Creator God who alone is worthy of worship and the false god who put himself in the place of God. The false god represents self-worship. The true God wants to free us from slavery and lead us to the promised land. The false god wants to keep us in bondage.

Is that a true picture of things, though? Does the true God indeed want to free us from slavery? If we follow God, are we not limited? Don't we then have to follow the restrictive morality imposed on us if we follow God? Isn't it true that the god of self-worship is in fact the way to freedom and to fulfillment and the path to self-discovery? If I follow my heart, am I not then free to discover who I am, free to find my own purpose in life, free to live by my own rules rather than to be subjected to the limiting rules of others, free to be whoever I choose to be?

Are we certain, though, that the freedoms involved in discovering ourselves will make us free? Or will they become a burden to us?

Culture observer and commentator Janie Cheaney wrote about her reaction to an article that reported on high schoolers raised in homes where the parents had undermined their children's idea that they are made in the image of a transcendent God and had replaced it with the idea that the children themselves are responsible for finding who they are in their true selves. It turns out that those children who are given the freedom to define themselves tend to suffer from high levels of anxiety. Such expectations cause the children of these parents to be anxious about having to define themselves. Here's Cheaney's reaction to what those children were experiencing: "Idols are heavy, whether gold or oak or personal identities. In these last days we've devised the heaviest of all: the burden of self. To tell adolescents 'You are enough,' 'You are perfect,' 'Follow your dream and live your truth' is to weigh them down with expectations they can't begin to meet."[1] Idols are indeed heavy, especially, as Cheaney writes, "the burden of self." We were never meant to carry the burden of defining ourselves but were instead meant to rest in God for who we are, having been made in his image. Kasey Leander, a writer for the Colson Center for Christian Worldview, said it well: "Our dominant philosophies tell us that each person is responsible for *creating* his or her own meaning out of an otherwise meaningless life."[2] Those words could also be applied to our identity and restated in this way: we are responsible for creating our identity out of an otherwise identity-less life.

Is creating meaning in a world that is without meaning a freedom or a burden? Is creating an identity in a world where we have no identity a freedom or a burden? Is defining our true self, when there is no idea what a true self is, a freedom or a burden?

To Whom Do We Belong?

In his book *You are Not Your Own*, Alan Noble writes that we are faced with two opposing attitudes toward life. The first is that we are our own and that we belong to ourselves. The second is that we are not our own and that we belong to God. The first attitude is the poiesis attitude where we look to our immanent selves for our identity and meaning. The second is the mimesis attitude where we look to the transcendent God for our identity and meaning.

Noble says that if we are our own and belong to ourselves, then there are at least four areas in which we have complete freedom of choice. First, we are free to define our identity, to declare who we are: "If I am my own and belong to myself, then I must define who 'I' am."[3] Second, we are free to choose what our meaning in life is: "If I am my own and belong to myself, then I am responsible for creating meaning in my life."[4] Third, we are free to choose our values: "If I am my own and belong to myself, then I'm also responsible for determining right and wrong. No other person or institution

---

1. Cheaney, "Things They Carry."
2. Stonestreet and Leander, "Gaslight Yourself"; emphasis in original.
3. Noble, *Not Your Own*, ch. 1.
4. Noble, *Not Your Own*, ch. 1.

has the authority to impose their morality on me."[5] Fourth, we are free to choose who we belong to: "If I am my own and belong to myself, then any and all associations, ties, and relationships I have are voluntary."[6]

Noble calls these choices the "Responsibilities of Self-Belonging."[7] It's significant that he calls them "responsibilities," not "freedoms." By using that term "responsibility," he's implying that the idea that "I am my own and belong to myself" might sound like it's a recipe for complete freedom and autonomy, but in fact, it's a responsibility that we carry on our shoulders that becomes, as he says, an "unbearable burden."[8]

Why, though, is "belonging to myself" an "unbearable burden?" Is that not one of the questions of this book? We're asking what is our true self and, as a result, what will most fulfill us and make us come alive: belonging to ourselves or belonging to God? Pharaoh, the created being who declared himself to be a god and who represents us as self-creators, wanted to keep the Israelites enslaved. God, the Creator of all things, on the other hand, wanted to free them from slavery and take them to the promised land. How, though, can belonging to God be more liberating than being like Pharaoh, who belonged to himself?

The answer is because we are more than ourselves. What I mean is that we are more than ourselves because we need a foundation outside ourselves. If we are only ourselves, then we can never find ourselves because there is nothing there to find. There is no foundation for our existence as persons, no foundation for meaning, no foundation for our identity, and no foundation for our belonging. There is only the endless attempt to create who we are without any foundation on which to build. Life takes on the endless task of attempting to create meaning without any foundation for meaning. We are constantly adrift with nothing to anchor us. To produce our own meaning is a burden because it has no foundation, nothing on which to ground it. If we produce our own purpose, we can never be certain that it is our true purpose, our final purpose, the purpose for which we were made, the purpose that reflects our true selves. Purpose can't be produced out of nothing; it must be given. Purpose that is received as a gift is a joy because we are then aligned with our being made in the image of the God who made us to reflect him and to be in a relationship with him.

5. Noble, *Not Your Own*, ch. 1.
6. Noble, *Not Your Own*, ch. 1.
7. Noble, *Not Your Own*, ch. 1.
8. Noble, *Not Your Own*, ch. 1.

DEFINING ONE'S TRUE SELF: A FREEDOM OR A BURDEN?

Augustine wrote that our souls have a "weight" that causes them to be driven toward that which will fulfill it. Here is how he describes it:

> A body inclines by its own weight towards the place that is fitting for it. Weight does not always tend towards the lowest place, but the one which suits it best, for though a stone falls, flame rises. Each thing acts according to its weight, finding its right level. If oil is poured into water, it rises to the surface, but if water is poured on to oil, it sinks below the oil. This happens because each acts according to its weight, finding its right level. When things are displaced, they are always on the move until they come to rest where they are meant to be.[9]

Augustine is talking about the weight of our souls and the nature of that to which our souls are inexorably drawn.

The image that comes to mind when I read Augustine's words is that of air bubbles as they are released from a scuba diver's breathing apparatus. Most of us have seen such an image. As the air bubbles travel up through the water, they quiver and shake as if they are consciously struggling to be united with the air above the water. That is their element; the place where they are meant to be, the place where they belong. Augustine is saying that our souls are like that in that there is an inexorable longing within our hearts that seeks with all its might to find its place of belonging, its place of fulfillment, the place where we are meant to be, the place where we are complete in our true selves because we are in relationship with the God who made us in his image.

Consider the rose, for example. The rose seed already contains the pattern—the rose image—within it even as a seed put there by the ultimate Designer. It grows into the fullness of the pattern for which it was intended. In the same way, we have the pattern of the image of God within us, but it is not yet fully realized or manifested. God's intention for us is that we would grow into that pattern. Just as a rose is most aligned with its true self when it becomes most fully a rose, so we will be most aligned with our true selves when we become most fully what God designed us to be, which is to be most fully human.

---

9. Augustine, *Confessions*, 13.9.

PART I: *DEFINING* ONE'S TRUE SELF

Work Versus Leisure

In his classic book *Leisure: The Basis of Culture*, German Catholic philosopher Josef Pieper argues against creating a culture that is based on "total work"[10] and in favor of one that is based on "leisure." What did he mean by that? Those terms—"total work" and "leisure"—need to be explained.

In a culture defined by "total work," the term "worker" does not refer to one's occupation or to the fact that capitalism is the foundation for the economy. Instead, "worker" refers to a concept of human being, or "man," whose entire life is being a functionary who produces, whose life consists of effort. Pieper writes, "The inmost significance of the exaggerated value which is set upon hard work appears to be this: man seems to mistrust everything that is effortless; he can only enjoy, with a good conscience, what he has acquired with toil and trouble; he refuses to have anything as a gift. . . . Man, from this point of view, is essentially a functionary, an official, even in the highest reaches of his activity."[11] The philosophy of "total work" that Pieper has in mind is the same as the immanent poietic philosophy of today where the self is that which is most important. Nothing exists beyond the horizontal concept of humanity; no God exists. There is no vertical, no gift of self from above. "Total work" is the secular philosophy where the material world is all there is. It's also the philosophy where we define ourselves. The idea of having knowledge in the culture of "total work" means that it "includes nothing which is not due to the effort of man, and there is nothing *gratuitous* about it, nothing 'inspired,' nothing 'given' about it."[12] We discover truth through reason alone; there is no sense in which truth is something that is revealed or given to us by God. We do not discover who we are because that implies that it's given. Instead, we create who we are. We do not discover meaning; we create meaning. We do not discover our values; we create our values. Such self-creation is what is meant by a culture of "total work."

Pieper contrasts that culture of "total work" with a culture of "leisure." He's not using the term "leisure" in the sense of taking time off from work. He explains that "leisure" used in that sense would still be related to work: "A break in one's work, whether of an hour, a day or a week, is still part of the world of work. . . . The pause is made for the sake of work and in order

---

10. Pieper, *Leisure*, ch. 1.
11. Pieper, *Leisure*, ch. 1.
12. Pieper, *Leisure*, ch. 1; emphasis in original.

to work, and a man is not only refreshed *from* work but *for* work."[13] Pieper is using "leisure" in the sense of the goodness of something being complete. We as human beings are good because God has made us complete in who we are. He explains, "We may read in the first chapter of Genesis that God 'ended his work which he had made' and 'behold, it was very good.' In leisure, man too celebrates the end of his work by allowing his inner eye to dwell for a while upon the reality of the Creation. He looks and he affirms: it is good."[14] Why is it good? Because it's complete. It has become aligned with the purpose for which it was made.

What is the hallmark of leisure? What is its essence? Its essence is celebration, having a festival: "Now the highest form of affirmation is the festival. . . . To hold a celebration means to affirm the basic meaningfulness of the universe and a sense of oneness with it, of inclusion within it. . . . And because leisure is thus by its nature a celebration, it is more than effortless; it is the direct opposite of effort."[15] What then is "leisure"? It's celebrating "the end of his work"! It's celebrating that God's work in us is complete. We are complete in our creation. Creation itself is complete. Nothing needs to be added. Our identity is complete. Our meaning is complete. Our belonging is complete. Leisure "is the direct opposite of effort." Instead, leisure is rest, fulfillment, being content in who we are. It is working from completeness, not toward completeness.

"Total work," on the other hand, says that we are the ones who must complete ourselves because we are incomplete. We are the ones who must create for ourselves our identity, our meaning, our values, our belonging. To find our true selves means we make and define ourselves. That means, though, that there is no place for resting in our being complete. Instead, it's a constant effort to define who we are, and that's a burden. The constant effort of attempting to, as in the words of Jesus, "find oneself" is wearing; it's a burden. To "lose ourselves," on the other hand, is to receive what God has given to us, which is that we are already made complete in his image. It's the opposite of making or defining ourselves.

By seeking to "find ourselves," we are rebelling against the idea that God has made us complete, and we are instead asserting that we make ourselves. When we make ourselves, though, we lose everything about ourselves. We even lose our personhood, as we saw with Chopra, Tolle, and Churchland.

---

13. Pieper, *Leisure*, ch. 3; emphasis in original.
14. Pieper, *Leisure*, ch. 3.
15. Pieper, *Leisure*, ch. 3.

Noble writes, on the other hand, that if I am not my own but belong to God, then our personhood has a real foundation for its existence:

> Your personhood is a real creation, objectively sustained by God. And as a creation of God, you have no obligation to create your self. Your identity is based on God's perfect will, not your own subjective, uncertain will. All your efforts to craft a perfect, marketable image add nothing to your personhood....
>
> This does not mean that you don't have a "true self." You do. But it is just not one that you are burdened with creating. We live as our true selves when we stand transparently before God, moment by moment.[16]

To live with utter dependence on God, which, as we will see, is one of the aspects of fearing God, we rest in God for all of who we are, including our existence, our identity, our values, our meaning, and our true selves. There is freedom and fulfillment in such utter dependence. Resting in who we are as made in the image of God is what will make us feel most alive. Why? Because it is who we were made to be; it is our true self.

The Burden of Freedom

Laura Perry Smalts's journey through transgenderism is an example of the burden of finding oneself when there is no foundation for that self except one's feelings. Laura had experienced several relationships with boys in which she had been rejected. She saw the power that boys had, and she envied that power: "Ever since I had been molested at the age of eight, I had felt cheated that men held the power in the relationship. This had been reinforced for over fifteen years every time I was dumped or men withheld sex. It was then that I began to determine in myself that I had to become a man."[17] She also felt that she had been born in the wrong body. In her mind she was male, but her body was female. She found a therapist who was willing to let her start hormone therapy, which caused her to feel that she was finally on the path to freedom: "Although I was thrilled about the path ahead of me, I was desperate to escape my female identity and found the early months of transition to be painfully slow. After a few months, though, my voice had lowered significantly, I was growing facial and body hair, and had much higher energy and sex drive. I

---

16. Noble, *Not Your Own*, ch. 5.
17. Smalts, *Transgender to Transformed*, ch. 7.

DEFINING ONE'S TRUE SELF: A FREEDOM OR A BURDEN?

was on cloud nine. I believed I was on the path to true freedom and lasting happiness."[18] Laura started wearing a chest binder, bought men's clothes, had a male-styled haircut, and changed her name to Jake. She also moved in with Steve, who was a transgender female, which meant that Steve was a male living as a female, and Laura was a female living as a male, so they were two transgender people in a heterosexual relationship but asserting themselves to be the opposite gender of their sex at birth.

Because Laura's chest binder started causing her back problems, she decided to have her breasts removed, bringing her one step closer to becoming a man. Before the surgery, though, she was afraid that she would not survive the surgery. After having not prayed in years, she cried out to God, "Please don't let me die. Please spare my life and let me wake up from this."[19]

She did survive the surgery and felt a sense of joy and fulfillment: "I couldn't believe the difference—my heavy chest suddenly felt so much lighter. I was on top of the world. I quickly forgot my cry to God and couldn't wait to finally fully embrace my male identity."[20]

For some reason, even though she thought she was the happiest she had ever been in her life, she was in fact depressed. Her boss noticed how she was unmotivated at work. Laura wasn't aware of her depression until her boss pointed it out. But why was she depressed? It was because deep down she realized, "I was no more a man than I had been prior to the surgery. I simply no longer had to wear chest binders."[21] Because she wasn't ready to give up on being a man, though, she had her female organs removed, thinking, "Surely having the female organs removed will make me more of a man. There will be nothing left to identify me as woman."[22] Even that didn't work, though. So she took the next step of finding a prosthetic penis that worked for her. The life of living as a transgender man became a burden. She was afraid when she went into men's bathrooms that she would be discovered. She even needed to watch what she said about her past, being sure to talk about "scouts" instead of "Girl Scouts." Laura wrote, "Dealing with the falseness of my identity had become exhausting. . . . The mounting reality of all the things I had to do differently

---

18. Smalts, *Transgender to Transformed*, ch. 7.
19. Smalts, *Transgender to Transformed*, ch. 7.
20. Smalts, *Transgender to Transformed*, ch. 7.
21. Smalts, *Transgender to Transformed*, ch. 8.
22. Smalts, *Transgender to Transformed*, ch. 8.

was beginning to crush my soul. . . . And I had to admit: though I was living as if I were male and everyone around me believed I was male, I was not truly happy. I had many happy moments, especially when I reached new milestones in transition. But, once I had transitioned as far as I could, I was left empty and broken."[23] What had started as a journey promising freedom to be who she was meant to be turned into a burden because there was no foundation beyond herself for her identity.

Laura came to believe in the claims of Christ and placed her faith in what he had done on her behalf. But she still thought she could live as a "man" of God. Laura became convicted, though, that she could not live that way. She wrote, "Laura was who he created; Jake had been my own creation, my own self-imposed identity, not His."[24] But that left her feeling condemned and hopeless. She knew that she could not be a woman, but "if God would not accept me as a man, where did that leave me?"[25] She wrote,

> As my heart sank even further and I was beginning to believe there was no hope, I heard the most loving voice I have ever heard in all my life whisper, "Let Me tell you who you are." I knew then that only God could define me, because He had created me. There was freedom in that. I had been running from God all my life trying to define myself, trying to discover who I was, when all along all I had to do was ask Him.[26]

Laura wrote that there was freedom in Jesus telling her who she was. Why? Because he gives us a foundation for who we are; he gives us an identity that is certain. She came alive when she rested in her God-given true self as having been made in the image of God.

Finding Rest in Reflecting God

The book of Genesis says that God made us in his image. Our true self, then, is found in our being made in the image of the God. As we locate our true self in our being made in the image of God, then we can be assured that we have value, identity, and meaning.

---

23. Smalts, *Transgender to Transformed*, ch. 8.
24. Smalts, *Transgender to Transformed*, ch. 8.
25. Smalts, *Transgender to Transformed*, ch. 8.
26. Smalts, *Transgender to Transformed*, ch. 8.

DEFINING ONE'S TRUE SELF: A FREEDOM OR A BURDEN?

Since God made us in his image, our relationship to him is like that of a painting to the artist who painted it. As is true of any artistic act, the thing created reflects its creator in that it reflects his or her thoughts, intentions, emotions, and personality. The painting becomes "fulfilled" as it aligns itself with the purpose for which it was made, which is to reflect those things of the artist. That's its purpose. We as humans are "the thing" created by our Creator, and therefore we reflect him. We are the piece of art created by God, the Artist. Just as a painting reflects the inner being of its painter, so we were made to reflect our Creator God. For us to say then that we can create our own true identity is the ultimate act of rebellion against God. Consider these words from Isaiah, one of the prophets in the Old Testament: "You turn things upside down, as if the potter were thought to be like the clay! Shall what is formed say to the one who formed it, 'You did not make me'? Can the [clay] pot say to the potter, 'You know nothing'?" (Isaiah 29:16). Just as it would be the height of pride for the clay pot to say such things to the one who formed it, so it is the height of pride for us to speak in such a way to our Creator.

Having been made in God's image means that we can rest in who we are. Because we are made in the image of the God who created us, then our identity is assured, guaranteed, secured, and certain. It's not dependent on the whims of human thought or ideology or on the dictates of some government. There is no greater or more firm a foundation for who we are than being made in the image of God who is ultimate. Being made in his image is the ultimate foundation for our value as persons, and that's true for three reasons.

First, it's foundational. Being made in God's image has to do with the essence of who we are. It's the most basic truth about us. Our identity as persons made in the image of God is more basic than our gender, race, nationality, family heritage, sexuality, intellectual abilities, or physical challenges.

Second, if we're made in the image of God, then our value as persons is unconditional. Other than being human, there are no conditions or characteristics that either qualify or disqualify us from being made in God's image. That means that there are no degrees of value between individuals; no person is more valuable than any other person.

Third, if we're made in the image of God, then our value as persons is secure. Since God is the foundation for our value as persons and since no one is more powerful than God, then no person, government, or ideology has the right to deny our value. There could not be a more secure foundation for our value as persons than our having been made in God's image. It is a gift from God that cannot be taken away.

By making ourselves in our own image, which is to say that we define who we are, we give up that security in who we are because we have given up the foundation for our identity.

The Rose That Chose to Become a Tree

If we refuse to live according to the image of God in which we were made and instead insist on defining ourselves, we will experience nothing but frustration, not fulfillment. Take the rose, again, as an example. Even as a seed, the rose has a blueprint within it that is the pattern for what it is meant to become. What, though, if the rose seed were to say, "I refuse to accept the arbitrary limitations imposed on me and instead assert my freedom to become whatever I want to be. Because I'm free to choose who I am and what my identity is, I choose to become a tree." What will happen to that rose? It will experience frustration, not freedom and fulfillment. Even more, it will experience alienation from itself and from the one who implanted the pattern within it. The Bible says that God created humankind in his image (Genesis 1:26). If we decide to create our own true self, then we are not only rejecting the blueprint in which God made us but also the Creator who put it there. Sin is becoming our own creator and rejecting the true Creator. Sin breaks the relationship between us and our Creator, which produces death, not life.

The God Who Knows Us

By creating us in his image, God not only gave us the blueprint of what would most fulfill us as we grow into that image, but he also did it so that we could be in a relationship with him, and he with us. When writing to the Christians in the ancient city of Galatia, the apostle Paul made the following statement: "But now that you know God—or rather are known by God" (Galatians 4:9). Paul was saying that the most important truth is not that we know God but that he knows us. David Benner takes that truth to its logical conclusion with this statement: "Knowing ourselves must . . . begin by knowing the self that is known by God. If God does not know us, we do not exist."[27] Again, "If God does not know us, we do not exist." Because God knows us, we matter; we have value. Our identity is found in him. Apart from him, we are nothing—literally. Our culture has placed so much importance on finding our true selves, but Benner is saying that unless God knows us, we do not even exist. If it is indeed true that the most important thing is that God knows us and that we do not exist apart from him, then the idea that we can find ourselves by defining our true selves is exposed as being an empty, even a deceitful, idea.

The God Who Turns Toward Us

You probably know Matthew Perry as the actor who played the character Chandler Bing in the popular TV series *Friends*. In his autobiography *Friends, Lovers, and the Big Terrible Thing: A Memoir*, Perry mentions an experience that left a deep impression on him and that caused him to feel, "*I'm not enough, I don't matter.*"[28] The experience had to do with the longing for his mother to notice him out of all the people surrounding her. He thought that if she would just turn and notice him out of all the people in the room, then he would know that he mattered to her:

> I vividly remember being at some fancy ballroom when I was about six years old, and when my mom came in, every head in the room turned. I wanted her to turn and look at me in these moments, but she was working and could not—it took me only thirty-seven years to work that out.
>
> Ever since then I have been addicted to "the turn." Once the turn happened, I could start making a woman laugh and making her want me sexually. Once the sex was done, reality set in, and I realized I didn't know these women at all. They were available, so I had no need for them. I had to get back out there and try to make them make the turn. That's why I slept with so many women. I was trying to re-create my childhood and win.[29]

What Perry was looking for with all those relationships was something he had not received from his mother. He was looking for "the turn." He was looking for his existence to be validated. He needed to know that he was enough, that he mattered. Well, God has turned not only to look at us

---

27. Benner, *Gift of Being Yourself*, 47.
28. Perry, *Friends*, ch. 1; emphasis in original.
29. Perry, *Friends*, ch. 3.

but also to know us, and by doing so, he has given us significance, value, meaning, existence, and hope. He is the one who makes us enough. Because of him, we matter. Because of him, we come alive. Because of him, we can rest in our true self.

Who Creates Reality?

There is a thought experiment in quantum physics known as Schrödinger's cat. It's a hypothetical experiment, so no real cat was injured in this experiment. The thought experiment consists of placing a cat inside a windowless box that contains radioactive material that is unpredictable as to whether or not it will disintegrate and send out an electron. If it does, the electron will start a mechanism that breaks a flask of poison that kills the cat. If it doesn't, the cat remains alive. According to quantum physics, both realities exist at the same time even though they are contradictory. It's not until a person opens the box and observes whether or not the cat is still alive that one of the two possibilities is made actual, made real. The conclusion of this thought experiment is that we who make the observation are the ones who actualize reality through our act of observation. The problem with this thought experiment, though, is that it does not take into account one very important factor, and that is that God is the ultimate observer. He is the one looking at his creation and making it real. When God looks at us, when God knows us, we become real. We are not the ones who make ourselves real. The God who is absolutely real and who is the ultimate observer is the one who makes us real, the one who brings all of creation into actuality. Benner continues, "[Christian theologian] J. I. Packer correctly captures the priority in all this knowing: 'What matters supremely, therefore, is not, in the last analysis, the fact that I know God, but the larger fact which underlies it—the fact that *he knows me*.' We are graven [written indelibly] on the palms of God's hands and never out of the Divine mind. All our knowledge of God depends on God's sustained initiative in knowing us. We know God, because God first knew us, and continues to know us."[30] We can be assured and fulfilled in who we are because our identity, our true self, is grounded in his image. He is the one who makes us real by turning toward us and knowing us.

---

30. Benner, *Gift of Being Yourself*, 47–48; emphasis in original.

DEFINING ONE'S TRUE SELF: A FREEDOM OR A BURDEN?

Questions for Personal Reflection or Group Discussion

1. Do you agree or disagree with the idea that defining, rather than discovering, our true selves is a burden? Why?
2. What does it mean to say that "we are more than ourselves"?
3. What are the advantages of living from the knowledge that we are complete in who we are because God made us in his image?
4. What do you think of the analogy that we are like paintings that were made to reflect the painter?
5. What is the significance of the idea that God knows us?
6. Do you think that God knows you? Why or why not?

PART II

Discovering One's True Self

We have just looked at the implications of the belief that we should follow our hearts and be true to ourselves. Such ideas are based on the idea that we have the freedom and the power to define who we are in our true selves.

Now we want to look at the belief that God has defined who we are and that we can discover who are in our true selves by looking outside ourselves at the God who made in his image. Focusing on God is what fearing God is all about. We will be fulfilled as we rest in the knowledge that we have been made in God's image and that we are therefore complete in who we are. There is no need to strive to find who we are; God has made his image known to us through Jesus Christ.

Fearing God: What It Means and What It Looks Like

4

Utter Dependence: Being Overwhelmed by Our Creator

THERE IS A REASON the Bible uses the word "fear" to describe how we should respond to God. Some understand the fear of God to mean a heightened sense of respect, reverence, or awe. Such words are certainly included in the concept of fear (see Psalm 102:15, Isaiah 59:18–19, Daniel 6:26), but those words are too tame when it comes to what the fear of God means. The fear of God should produce in us an intensity, an urgency, and a sense of being utterly overwhelmed by and dependent on God. To fear something means that it captures our attention and confronts us with a need to act, which is precisely the response that is warranted by the almighty God. Fear is not a take-it-or-leave-it experience; it is both confrontational and immediate. It causes one to face that which is undeniably real, that which is beyond our control, and that which is unavoidable. While the concepts of awe, respect, and reverence are fine as far as they go, they don't go far enough. They fail to communicate as adequately as the word "fear" the sense of intensity, of immediacy, and of being overwhelmed by and dependent on the absolutely real and infinite God.

The God who is to be feared is not to be taken lightly. Consider what the Lord told Jeremiah: "Should you not *fear* me? . . . Should you not *tremble* in my presence" (Jeremiah 5:22, emphasis added). Then, too, Job, after speaking of how no one could thwart the will of God, says, "That is why I am *terrified* of him; when I think of all this, I *fear* him" (Job 23:15, emphasis added). The psalmist wrote, "My flesh trembles in fear of you" (Psalm

119:120). To fear God is not merely a sense of being frightened or startled, but a long and deep sense of danger. When Isaiah encountered the presence of the absolutely holy God in the temple, he said, "Woe to me! . . . I am ruined!" (Isaiah 6:5). Those words convey a dreadful fear. When the apostle John saw the One whose "eyes were like blazing fire" and whose "feet were like bronze glowing in a furnace," he "fell at his feet as though dead" (Revelation 1:14–15, 17). The proper response to such a God is indeed that of fear, not merely awe, reverence, or respect.

God told Moses, "No one can see my face, for no one may see me and live" (Exodus 33:20). While the word "fear" is not contained in the words, the meaning of fear is definitely there. God's words to Moses convey God's complete and total otherness. This is consistent with the primary meaning of the word "holy," which means to be separate, set apart, and other. The idea that God is totally other is powerfully conveyed in Isaiah 6 where the word "holy" is repeated three times: "Holy, holy, holy is the LORD Almighty" (Isaiah 6:3). Repetition in Hebrew poetry communicates importance and significance, and repeating the word "holy" three times means his otherness is extremely important and significant.

Fear also conveys otherness because the experience of fear draws our attention away from ourselves and onto the object of fear, which is outside us. This otherness of God conveys the sense that there is an absoluteness to the reality and the being of God. God is absolute in his reality. The reality of God's existence is the foundation for the reality of all else, of all created things.

What then is the core meaning of fearing God? I could cite several verses,[1] but I will quote only this one simple verse: "It is you [God] alone who are to be feared" (Psalm 76:7). The core meaning of fearing God is to acknowledge that God alone is God. There are no other gods. God alone is worthy of our worship, worthy of being feared. Why is that? The following psalm explains: "For great is the LORD and most worthy of praise; / he is

---

1. "Fear the LORD your God, serve him only and take your oaths in his name. Do not follow other gods" (Deuteronomy 6:13–14); "It is the LORD your God you must follow, and him you must revere [fear]. Keep his commands and obey him; serve him and hold fast to him" (Deuteronomy 13:4); "Now fear the LORD and serve him with all faithfulness. Throw away the gods your forefathers worshiped beyond the River and in Egypt, and serve the LORD" (Joshua 24:14–15); "For great is the LORD and most worthy of praise; he is to be feared above all gods" (1 Chronicles 16:25); "No one is like you, LORD; you are great, and your name is mighty in power. Who should not fear you, King of the nations? This is your due. Among all the wise leaders of the nations and in all their kingdoms, there is no one like you" (Jeremiah 10:6–7).

to be feared above all gods. / For all the gods of the nations are idols, / but the LORD made the heavens" (Psalm 96:4-5). We should fear God alone because he created all things; he's our Creator. The following psalm connects fearing God with him being our Creator directly: "Let all the earth fear the Lord; / let all the people of the world revere him. / For he spoke, and it came to be" (Psalm 33:8-9). A similar message is given in the book of Revelation: "Fear God and give him glory. . . . Worship him who made the heavens, the earth, the sea and the springs of water" (Revelation 14:7).

Psalm 33:8-9 and verses like it are fundamental to what it means to fear God. Why should we fear God? Because "he spoke, and it came to be." What that means is that God created all things by his infinitely powerful word, and he did so without using any preexisting matter or energy. He created space and time out of nothing. Before God created the universe, only he existed. When God spoke his words of creation, the universe came into existence out of nothing. This doctrine is called *creatio ex nihilo* ("creation out of nothing"). We should fear God because he alone is our Creator, which makes him the only God worthy of our worship and of our being overwhelmed by him. In the book of Isaiah, God declares, "Has not my hand made all these things, and so they came into being?" (Isaiah 66:2). In Revelation, the last book of the Bible, it is written, "You are worthy, our Lord and God, to receive glory and honor and power, for you created all things, and by your will they were created and have their being" (Revelation 4:11).

The fact that God created us out of nothing means that there is an unbridgeable and infinite gap between the being of God and our being. God did not create us by extending his being into our being like a stream that flows from a lake where the waters of the lake and the stream are of the same essence. There is no extension of some spiritual force of being between us and God. The difference between us and God in regard to our being could not be greater. God's being is necessary; ours is contingent. We did not have to exist; God does have to exist. We exist only because God spoke us into existence. God is the unmoved Mover, the uncaused Cause. We are the effect of his creative and causal activity. Theologian Matthew Barrett expands on the difference between us and God by saying that

> God is not just a greater being than us, as if he were merely different in *degree*, a type of superman. No, this God is different in *kind*. He is a different type of being altogether. He is the Creator, not the created. From this fundamental difference—what theologians

have called the Creator-creature distinction—every other difference follows.... There is no one like God. He is, as Isaiah 40:28 says, "unsearchable." That word "unsearchable" is key. It's not only true that God is incomparable, but he is also incomprehensible. His power, his knowledge, his presence, and his wisdom are inexhaustible and unfathomable. No one ever has known, and no one ever will know, the depths of his essence, the scope of his might, or the height of his glory. He is, in a word, *infinite*. That we cannot say of anyone else. "I am God, and there is none like me" (Isa. 46:9).[2]

Not only did God create us out of nothing, but he also sustains us in our existence from moment to moment. The author of the book of Hebrews wrote that God is "sustaining all things by his powerful word" (Hebrews 1:3). Each moment of every day we—and the universe—are sustained in our existence by the free, sovereign, and powerful word of God.

Utterly Dependent

What does our being created out of nothing and sustained in our existence moment by moment mean for us? It means that we are utterly dependent on God for our very existence. Theologian Norman Geisler wrote, "Creation is utterly dependent on God; this dependence applies to creation's present status as well as to its past status. The universe and everything in it began as God's creation and it continues to be God's creation. God is the originating Cause as well as the sustaining Cause of everything that exists."[3] How should our being utterly dependent on God for having created us and for continuing to sustain us affect us? It should overwhelm and humble us. It should cause us to bow down before our Creator and give him all our praise, glory, and thanks. The psalmist wrote, "Praise the LORD, my soul; / *all my inmost being*, praise his holy name" (Psalm 103:1, emphasis added). We should praise God with all of who we are—with "all my inmost being"—because we are overwhelmed by him.

Fulfilled Through Fear

Being overwhelmed by God in a healthy, fulfilling sense is what fearing God is all about. Pastor Timothy Keller and his wife, Kathy, define the fear

2. Barrett, *None Greater*, 21–22; emphasis in original.
3. Geisler, *God, Creation*, 500.

UTTER DEPENDENCE: BEING OVERWHELMED BY OUR CREATOR

of God in this way: "'Fear' in the Bible means to be overwhelmed, to be controlled by something. To fear the Lord is to be overwhelmed with wonder before the greatness of God and his love."[4]

The power of nature has a way of humbling and overwhelming us. Some of us have been humbled and overwhelmed by the brightness of the flash and the loudness of the clap of thunder when lightning struck close by. I remember being humbled by the power of an earthquake that caused the Jack in the Box I was working in to sway for more than a minute—but it seemed like forever. The floor beneath my feet rolled up and down. That experience of instability shook me to my core.

While being overwhelmed by the power of nature causes us to be afraid, being overwhelmed by the power of God has the opposite effect; it fulfills us. It makes us come alive. Professor Grant Horner wrote, "For a believer, fearing God is a sublime, deep pleasure. That is what the ultimate fear is—pleasurable. It is not supposed to be negative, uncomfortable, or debilitating, but rather edifying by showing us who and what we are in terms of an almighty and infinite being."[5] Why is fearing God fulfilling and pleasurable? Because God made us that way. He made us to be fulfilled as we are in relationship with him. To be fulfilled by knowing the infinite God reflects who we are as having been made in the image of God, which is our true self, and fearing God flows out from that true self. God made us with an infinity-sized hole that can be filled only by the infinite God himself. Seventeenth-century French mathematician and religious thinker Blaise Pascal wrote that "this infinite abyss [inside us] can be filled only with an infinite and immutable object; in other words by God himself."[6] We were made to fear God, and we will be most fulfilled and will come alive when we live in a relationship with the God who is to be feared.

An Experiment About What Makes Life Fulfilling

The Old Testament book of Ecclesiastes tells the story of how King Solomon performed an experiment. He wanted to see if life would be satisfying when living for only the things of the world and having no thought of God in mind. He immersed himself in pleasure, in building projects, in gaining wealth, and in enjoying the arts. What he found was that "when

---

4. Keller and Keller, *Meaning of Marriage*, 68.
5. Horner, *Meaning at the Movies*, 6.
6. Pascal, *Pensées*, 75.

[he] surveyed all that [his] hands had done and what [he] had toiled to achieve, everything was meaningless, a chasing after the wind; nothing was gained under the sun" (Ecclesiastes 2:11). He discovered what will not fulfill us. What, though, did he conclude will fulfill us? He concluded that we are meant to fear God: "Now all has been heard; here is the conclusion of the matter: Fear God and keep his commandments, for this is the duty of all mankind" (Ecclesiastes 12:13). The word "duty" in that verse makes fearing God sound like a joyless obligation. In truth, though, it is a duty because to fear God is how he made us, and to live according to how God made us brings joy and fulfillment because it fulfills our primary purpose in life. It is the duty, for example, of a rose seed to become a rose because that is its nature, its true self, the pattern inside it that becomes manifested. But a rose growing into the fullness of all its beauty is also its joy. We have a duty to live according to how God made us, but that is also our joy, our purpose. By doing so, we will be most fulfilled and will come most alive because it is who we were made to be.

Overwhelmed by God

Yes, fearing God will fulfill us because he made us that way, but why exactly is that fulfilling? It's fulfilling because fearing God means being overwhelmed by him, and we are most fulfilled and most alive when we are overwhelmed by a passion for God. That's true because there is a deep longing that lies within our hearts. It's the longing to be overwhelmed with a passion for something, and that longing to be overwhelmed by a passion for God is what fearing God is all about.

We want to be consumed by something. We want to give our lives to something that overcomes us. If we're honest with ourselves, we're not satisfied when living only lukewarm lives; we want to be consumed by a passion for something. Being overwhelmed is what gives our lives meaning, excitement, and vibrancy. Author John Eldredge writes about how desire is essential to who we are: "It's not that we have desire—we are desire. Desire is the essence of the human soul, the secret of our existence."[7] Desire is not just something added to us; it is an essential part of our nature. It flows from who we are. What is desire but a longing to be overwhelmed, to be consumed by a passion for something? It's a craving. That longing to be overwhelmed flows out of who we are, and we will not come alive until

7. Eldredge, *Dare to Desire*, 20.

we are overwhelmed by a passion for our Creator God who made us in his image. The psalmist wrote, "He fulfills the desires of those who fear him" (Psalm 145:19). Theologian Thaddeus Williams says it well when he writes,

> We were made to revere Someone infinitely more interesting than ourselves. . . . It is in a state of self-forgetful reverence that we become most truly and freely ourselves. . . . The more self-absorbed we are, the less awe we experience; the less awe we experience, the less fully ourselves we become. . . . The more you revere [read: fear] something more awesome than yourself, the more alive you become. The more you revere yourself as the most awesome being in existence, the more awful [in the sense of meaningless] your life becomes.[8]

Jesus' Passion for God

If I could boil the message of this book down to one image, it would be the story of Jesus clearing out the temple courts because he had an overwhelming passion that God alone be worshiped. Here's the story.

One day Jesus entered the temple in Jerusalem with his disciples where he encountered the noise of cattle and the chaos of the merchants exchanging money and selling animals for sacrifice. He became so enraged by the disruptive nature of what was happening that he made a whip with whatever cords were available, overturned the tables, and drove out the cattle and the merchants. Here's the passage: "In the temple courts [Jesus] found men selling cattle, sheep and doves, and others sitting at tables exchanging money. So he made a whip out of cords, and drove all from the temple area, both sheep and cattle; he scattered the coins of the money changers and overturned their tables. To those who sold doves he said, 'Get these out of here! Stop turning my Father's house into a market!' His disciples remembered that it is written: 'Zeal for your house will consume me'" (John 2:14–17).

It's true that the merchants were providing a service for those who had to travel long distances to worship at the temple in Jerusalem and that it was difficult transporting animals without causing them to be blemished. But the merchants were often swindling the worshipers, disqualifying their animals for the most minor of reasons. Another problem was that this business was taking place in the court of the gentiles, which

---

8. Williams, *Don't Follow Your Heart*, ch. 1.

meant that the gentiles who had come to worship were forced to do so in the midst of the noise and the chaos.[9] It's clear, though, that what most upset Jesus was that the place that was supposed to be devoted to worshiping God was being disrupted: "Zeal for your house will consume me!" Jesus was consumed by a passion that God be worshiped. This passion that God be worshiped overwhelmed him. That's why he cleared out the chaos and the noise in the temple.

Zeal Characterized Jesus' Entire Life

Jesus' zeal for fearing and worshiping God was something that was true not only during that single incident at the temple, but it characterized his entire life. His life is an example of what it means to live with an overwhelming sense of being utterly dependent on God. Amazingly, Jesus, who, being God, had life in himself,[10] "temporarily suspended"[11] the use of some of his divine attributes without giving up his divine nature as God, and he became a man. Paul wrote, "Though [Jesus] was God, he did not think of equality with God as something to cling to. Instead, he gave up his divine privileges" (Philippians 2:6–7 NLT). Why did he do this? There are several important reasons, but the one we want to focus on here is that he wanted to show how we are to live in utter dependence on the overwhelming God. The following verses speak of the utter dependence that Jesus had on the Father:

- "Very truly I tell you, the Son can do nothing by himself; he can only do what he sees his Father doing" (John 5:19).
- "I do nothing on my own but speak just what the Father has taught me" (John 8:28).
- "The words I say to you I do not speak on my own authority. Rather, it is the Father, living in me, who is doing his work" (John 14:10).

What did it mean for Jesus to live in utter dependence on God? As indicated by the above verses, it meant to live with an overwhelming passion for God. To "do nothing by himself" but to do only "what he sees his Father

---

9. Barton et al., *Luke*, 444–45.
10. "For as the Father has life in himself, so he has granted the Son also to have life in himself" (John 5:26).
11. Groothuis, *Christian Apologetics*, 565.

doing" are words of being overwhelmed by a passion for his Father. That's how Jesus lived, and he calls for us to live in that way as well.

Clearing Out the Temple of Our Lives

How is the story of Jesus clearing out the temple relevant to us? I mentioned that if I could distill what it means to fear God into a single story, it would be Jesus clearing out the temple. Why do I see that story as being so significant? What Jesus did in the temple is what he wants to do in our lives. He wants to clear out all the noise, the chaos, the false selves, the false gods, and the fruitless distractions from our lives and replace them with an overwhelming passion to worship the God who is to be feared, the God who overwhelms. He wants to clear those things out from our lives so that we be fulfilled by losing ourselves in a passion for the living God. To lose ourselves in an all-consuming passion for the living God is what we were made for; it's our core purpose in life.

How, though, can he do that? Let me answer that question with a question. How does God give us eternal life? Does he simply grant us eternal life? No, we *receive* eternal life by receiving the very presence of God in us through the Holy Spirit who takes up residence within our lives. Just as God resided in the physical temple in Jerusalem, so now, as we place our faith in Jesus, we become the new temple as the Holy Spirit, the very presence of God, resides within us. We don't become God—the infinite separation between his being and our being remains between us—but the Holy Spirit dwells within us and makes our spirit come to life so that the relationship between us and God is restored. The Holy Spirit clears out death from our lives and makes it a living temple where we can worship and serve the living God. He transforms us from being spiritually dead to being spiritually alive. This relationship with God is what we were made for. Paul writes about the work of the Holy Spirit in the following verses. As you read these verses, look for the word "governed" and be aware of how it is used:

> The mind governed by the flesh is death, but the mind governed by the Spirit is life and peace. The mind governed by the flesh is hostile to God; it does not submit to God's law, nor can it do so. Those who are in the realm of the flesh cannot please God.

> You, however, are not in the realm of the flesh but are in the realm of the Spirit, if indeed the Spirit of God lives in you. And if anyone

does not have the Spirit of Christ, they do not belong to Christ. But if Christ is in you, then even though your body is subject to death because of sin, the Spirit gives life because of righteousness. And if the Spirit of him who raised Jesus from the dead is living in you, he who raised Christ from the dead will also give life to your mortal bodies because of his Spirit who lives in you. (Romans 8:6–11)

Paul uses the word "governed" three times in the above passage: once to talk about being governed by our sinful nature and twice to talk about being governed by the Holy Spirit. To be governed is to be overwhelmed by something, which is what fear is all about. To be governed by the Holy Spirit is to allow him to transform our lives in a way that is not possible for us to do in our own power. The Christian life is one of finding rest through utter dependence, and our utter dependence is on the Holy Spirit of God who resides within us and gives us new life.

To the Christians who were part of the church in the city of Corinth (in present-day Turkey), the apostle Paul wrote, "Do you not know that your bodies are temples of the Holy Spirit, who is in you, whom you have received from God? You are not your own; you were bought at a price" (1 Corinthians 6:19–20). When Paul wrote, "Your bodies are temples of the Holy Spirit," he was referring to each individual believer. The "your" is plural, and "bodies" in the original Greek is singular, meaning "each individual body," where "body" refers to an individual person.[12] Each individual believer is a temple of God because they have the Holy Spirit—the Spirit of God—residing within them, transforming them, clearing out the old gods that lead to death within them, making them a new creation that is alive to God, and stirring within them an overwhelming passion for the living God.

The Holy Spirit works in us to give us the power to clear out all the things in our lives that take our focus off God, that enslave us, and that cause us to be afraid of God. The Holy Spirit does this by giving us the assurance that we are now part of God's family to such an extent that we now feel free to call God the equivalent of "Dad." Paul writes, "The Spirit you received does not make you slaves, so that you live in fear again; rather, the Spirit you received brought about your adoption to sonship. And by him we cry, 'Abba, Father.' The Spirit himself testifies with our spirit that we are God's children." (Romans 8:15–16). "Abba" was a term implying intimacy in a relationship with one's father, a term of endearment.[13]

---

12. Blomberg, *1 Corinthians*, 127.
13. Dyck, *Yawning at Tigers*, 129.

Unbecoming?

Doesn't it seem rather unbecoming, though, for God to create us so that we would fear him where fear means to glorify and to worship him? Does that not come across as rather self-serving and self-adulating? Is God a needy God that he needed to create us so that he would have someone to glorify and worship him?

God did not create us, though, because he had a need to be glorified. Instead, he created us so that *we* would be fulfilled and come alive as we glorify and worship him. We need to understand that God does nothing out of a selfish motivation. He does everything for us. The desire to give is in the very nature of God.

The greatest evidence of God's giving nature is how God the Father gave his Son Jesus Christ: "For God so loved the world that *he gave* his one and only Son, that whoever believes in him shall not perish but have eternal life" (John 3:16, emphasis added). After we broke our relationship with him, God sent his Son, Jesus, to restore that relationship, and he did so while we were still in rebellion against him: "But God demonstrates his own love for us in this: *While we were still sinners*, Christ died for us" (Romans 5:8, emphasis added). Yes, God created us so that he would be glorified through us, but he did not need our glorification or our worship of him. He is entirely complete in himself. He does nothing out of a need to be more complete. Whatever God does, he does for the sake of others. He created us to glorify him because *we* are the ones who would be fulfilled when we glorify and fear him. We were made to fear and glorify God, and until we do, we will not be all that we were meant to be.

An Eternal Tension

There is an interesting tension that our yearning to be fulfilled through a passion for the overwhelming God raises within us. It's the tension between being completely satisfied while, at the same time, wanting more. Stephen Turley calls this tension the "eternal dynamic":

> The key characteristic of this stretching out of the soul toward God is its eternal dynamic: given the Goodness of God in His infinity, there is no end in this longing, for no matter how much one is filled with divine Beauty, one longs for more. The eternal dynamic of epektasis [an intense desire or longing], however, should not be

confused with a frustrated soul, since the eternal longing for ever more divine glory is itself the fruit of the satisfaction that the soul experiences in its encounter with the divine Beauty.[14]

Turley is saying that we are to be eternally attracted to God, and as we are, we will be simultaneously both satisfied and dissatisfied. That dissatisfaction, though, should not be understood as stemming from a frustration of never being fully satisfied, but instead it should be seen as the fruit of the satisfaction of knowing God. The more we know God, the more we want to know him. To understand this tension between being fully satisfied while simultaneously wanting more, imagine an extremely healthy marriage where the husband and wife are fully satisfied in their relationship with each other, and yet the more they get to know each other, the more they want their intimate knowledge of each other to go even deeper.

By way of a summary, we looked at the verse that said, "Let all the earth fear the LORD; / let all the people of the world revere him. / For he spoke, and it came to be" (Psalm 33:8–9). Why should we fear God? Because he created us from nothing. How should that affect us? It should humble us and cause us to realize that we are utterly dependent in him for our existence. Utter dependence is the first of the three aspects as to what it looks like to fear God.

Questions for Personal Reflection or Group Discussion

1. What is the core meaning of fearing God?
2. Do you agree that we are utterly dependent on God? Why or why not?
3. Do you see being utterly dependent on God as a good thing or a bad thing?
4. How should our utter dependence on God affect us when it comes to what it means to fearing God?
5. Why is fearing God fulfilling?
6. What is the "eternal dynamic"? What do you think about that idea?

---

14. Turley, *Awakening Wonder*, ch. 3.

5

Undivided Attention: Come Alive by Focusing on God

The mission was to record the weather at the South Pole for the purpose of discerning the effects that the weather at that extreme part of the globe had on the rest of the Southern Hemisphere. Such a mission required that a station be set up at the South Pole and that someone live there for seven months in order to record the changes and patterns in the weather. Admiral Richard Byrd volunteered to be that person.[1]

The hut in which Byrd stayed was small and had no view because it was dark for twenty-four hours a day for six of the seven months Byrd occupied the station. Moreover, it was terribly difficult for a person to take a walk outside because the temperature usually ranged from forty to seventy degrees Fahrenheit below zero. Then, too, the snow was often blowing, which cut down on visibility.

Still, Byrd found that he absolutely had to venture outside his hut once a day so as to break the monotony of the routine and to get the little amount of exercise that he could. To ensure that he could find his way back to the hut, he carried a bundle of bamboo sticks and planted one in the snow every three steps. This was necessary because when he got any distance at all from his hut, the featureless landscape looked the same in every direction. Also, the snow would drift over his hut, which had been constructed partially underground, causing it to be indistinguishable from every other mound of snow in the area.

---

1. The overview of this story draws from Byrd's account in Byrd, *Alone*, 116–18.

PART II: *DISCOVERING ONE'S TRUE SELF*

Byrd would use these daily walks to escape the bleakness of his situation. As he walked, he would imagine that he was on a walk with his wife in Boston or that he was a member of the voyage with Marco Polo. One day, though, he became so caught up in his thoughts that he walked beyond the line of his bamboo sticks. When he finally came out of his mental escape, he realized that he did not know the way back to the hut, and his footprints had left no mark in the hard-packed snow, called "sastrugi." He did remember that the wind had been blowing on his left cheek when he started on his walk, and it was still blowing on his left. But that meant very little since the wind was constantly shifting directions, and he might have shifted the direction in which he had been walking as the direction of the wind had changed.

As a result, Byrd was without a reference point as to where his hut was located. He had no idea in which direction he should walk to return to the warmth and safety of his hut. By now, the clouds had covered the stars. He was lost, and he had no idea whether his next step would take him closer to his hut or farther away. Byrd was entirely alone and completely lost. A sense of panic rose within him.

To establish a reference point, he chipped out chunks of the sastrugi with his boots and built an eighteen-inch-high mound. He also discovered two stars that were shining through a break in the clouds, and those two stars were in alignment with the direction in which he thought he had been walking. He lined himself up with the two stars and headed to what he hoped was back to the hut. He walked one hundred steps and did not see the line of bamboo sticks. Then he looked back and shone his flashlight to see if he could locate the pile of sastrugi. Panic rose within him again when he couldn't locate that small mound of ice. So, he retraced the one hundred steps and found the mound around twenty feet to his left. Starting again from the pile of sastrugi, he set out on another course around thirty degrees to the left. He went another hundred steps and still saw no sign of the bamboo sticks. Byrd built another mound of sastrugi there and decided to continue another thirty paces in the same direction. On the twenty-ninth step, he came across the line of bamboo sticks. Byrd wrote later, "No shipwrecked mariner, sighting a distant sail, could have been more overjoyed."[2]

In himself, Byrd would have been lost. He needed to fix his attention on the mounds of sastrugi and the two stars to find his way back to the safety and warmth of the hut. For the sake of survival, he focused on them.

2. Byrd, *Alone*, 118.

UNDIVIDED ATTENTION: COME ALIVE BY FOCUSING ON GOD

Why did I tell this story? It's a metaphor for our lives. Having a fixed point outside us is a matter of survival. Byrd knew he was lost and needed a fixed point outside himself to find his way back to the safety of the hut. Byrd would have died if he had continued to focus on his mental escape from the bleakness of the surrounding reality. We, too, are lost if we persist in focusing on ourselves. We need to fix our attention on something outside ourselves not only so that we can survive, but also to know who we are and what our purpose is. The God who is to be feared does that; he gives us that fixed point. Just as Byrd found safety by focusing his full attention on those fixed points outside himself, so we will find fulfillment as we give God our undivided attention.

What Fear and Love Share in Common

There is an interesting juxtaposition of two seemingly conflicting phrases in Deuteronomy: "And now, Israel, what does the LORD your God ask of you but to fear the LORD your God, to walk in obedience to him, to love him, to serve the LORD your God with all your heart and with all your soul" (Deuteronomy 10:12). In this verse, God is asking us both to fear him and to love him. How is that possible? Fear and love seem to be conflicting emotions. There is something that both fear and love have in common, though. It's undivided attention.

What does fear do to us? It demands our attention. Fear is not a take-it-or-leave-it experience. Love is different in that we want to give our undivided attention to that which we love.

We see the kind of God who is worthy of being both feared and loved in the biblical passage where the prophet Isaiah describes his experience in the temple: "In the year that King Uzziah died, I saw the Lord, high and exalted, seated on a throne; and the train of his robe filled the temple. Above him were seraphim, each with six wings: With two wings they covered their faces, with two they covered their feet, and with two they were flying. And they were calling to one another: 'Holy, holy, holy is the LORD Almighty; the whole earth is full of his glory'" (Isaiah 6:1–3). The word "seraphim," which is a type of angel, can be translated as "burning ones."[3] Since fire normally destroys things, one would think that angels made of fire would be indestructible. And yet these fiery beings need to cover their faces when they look directly at the unmediated glory of God.

3. Motyer, *Prophecy of Isaiah*, 76.

Even though the seraphim are confronted with this dangerous God, they don't run away. Why not? What would cause these fiery beings to be so enthralled with this God who is so dangerous that even they can't withstand his unmediated glory? It's God's "splendor." As David wrote in the psalm, "Worship the Lord in the splendor of his holiness; / tremble before him, all the earth" (Psalm 96:9). That verse contains both the fear of God ("tremble") and the beautiful splendor of God. God's splendor is dangerous, and it causes us to not only to have a healthy fear of him but also to be enthralled with him. What is "splendor"? It's beauty with the added elements of grandeur, magnificence, and majesty. Splendor is overwhelming beauty. It's a beauty that is so majestic, it scares us.

Consider the following experiment that took place in a busy subway station. The experiment was designed by the *Washington Post* to test whether beauty would capture the attention of those who were going about their busy lives. The question they posed was, "In a banal setting at an inconvenient time, would beauty transcend?" The setting was the L'Enfant Plaza in Washington, DC. The time was eight o'clock in the morning. The musician was an unexceptional-looking young man wearing casual clothes and standing by a wall next to a trash can. He happened to be, though, a virtuoso violin player named Joshua Bell "whose talents can command $1,000 a minute." The violin was "handcrafted in 1713 by Antonio Stradivari during the Italian master's 'golden period'" and worth millions of dollars. The music was not familiar popular tunes, but less-familiar, beautiful, classical pieces. Out of the 1,097 people who passed by, how many do you think stopped for even a minute to listen to this virtuoso play his beautiful music? Seven! Gene Weingarten, the reporter who reported on this event, asked, "If we can't take the time out of our lives to stay a moment and listen to one of the best musicians on Earth play some of the best music ever written; if the surge of modern life so overpowers us that we are deaf and blind to something like that—then what else are we missing?"[4] That's a good question. I don't think, however, that the experiment was adequate for testing what they were looking for. No matter how skilled Joshua Bell was, how valuable the violin was, or how beautiful the music was, it was no surprise that the music didn't stand a chance of capturing the commuters' attention because they were, understandably, too distracted by other things. Perhaps we need to learn from this experiment that the hectic nature of life can cause us to fail to appreciate the beauty

---

4. Quotes here and preceding from Weingarten, "Pearls Before Breakfast."

around us; but if those conducting this experiment had wanted to design a more valid test, I would suggest the following change to their experiment. Make the music more like Isaiah's experience in the temple where the music would have shaken the walls, the floors, and the columns of the subway station to the point where the commuters would have feared for their lives. That kind of dangerous splendor would have certainly gotten their attention. If you add danger to splendor, then ignoring it becomes a matter of our intentionally suppressing it. Having made that revision to the experiment, then it becomes relevant to all of us because then we need to ask ourselves the question, Do we realize that we live every moment in the context of a God who is to be feared because of his dangerous splendor, and yet we still fail to give him our undivided attention?

Scared to Death

Speaking of dangerous splendor, Half Dome is a huge geological formation that rises almost a mile (five thousand feet) above the floor of Yosemite Valley. It strikes both awe and fear in anyone who views it across the valley from Glacier Point. It's an excellent example of what dangerous splendor does to us because it causes people to be both fearful of it and drawn to it. Mark Galli writes, "When we go to places like Glacier Point, we find ourselves attracted to the very thing that makes us afraid. And rather than running from it, we want to get closer, at least as close as we can without getting killed."[5] Galli says that the same is true of God: "When people witness the power and the glory of the almighty God, they are terrified. They think they are going to die. When we blithely sing to God to 'show us your glory, Lord,' we might as well be making a death wish. Or maybe we just want to get close to something that scares us to death."[6]

That's what God's dangerous splendor should do to us. It should cause to be so enthralled with God's beauty that we can't stop looking at him. At the same time, it should scare us to death.

---

5. Galli, "Fear That Draws Us," 48.
6. Galli, "Fear That Draws Us," 48.

PART II: *DISCOVERING* ONE'S TRUE SELF

Danger Has Its Place

There is a place for danger in our lives. Controlled danger makes us come alive. Don Dyck wrote about a time when he, his wife, and their baby took a vacation at a four-star hotel in Hawaii. One of the features of the hotel was that it had a man-made lagoon filled with colorful tropical fish. One day he and his wife took turns swimming across the lagoon while the other parent watched the baby. While they were thrilled swimming across the lagoon and viewing all the colorful fish the first few times, after awhile they got bored. Dyck writes,

> The problem really wasn't what was in the lagoon. It's what wasn't. There were no waves, no spray from the surf, no tides, no coral reefs, no danger, no depths.
>
> I believe there's a spiritual equivalent to that man-made lagoon. If the ocean is like God, the lagoon is a poor, but useful, replacement. . . . It's engagement with a lesser deity. . . . It's a life designed to give us spiritual experiences while cushioning us from the reality of a dangerous God.
>
> Just like the man-made lagoon had real ocean water and marine life, this "god lagoon" may contain some spiritual truths. We may even encounter qualities of the true God—but only the ones we deem acceptable. Divine characteristics we find threatening or that clash with our modern sensibilities, we carefully screen out. Life in the lagoon means never being surprised by God. . . . Ultimately, it means we are in control.[7]

When we think of what it means to be fulfilled, we tend to think of it in terms of something that is calm. Perhaps we think of sitting safely at home enjoying a delicious meal and having good conversation with friends. Or perhaps being fulfilled makes one think of merely being content and at peace with oneself. Those feelings are true and fine as far as they go, but being fulfilled by fearing God goes far beyond such peaceful and calm images to something much more wild. Being fulfilled through fearing God is both peaceful and wild at the same time. It's being so enamored with the overwhelming majesty of God mixed with the feeling baby chicks must have when they are huddled safely under their mother's wings. When we live with both the safety and the danger of God, then we live in the fullness of life. Living in the context of the beautiful but dangerous God is what we

---

7. Dyck, *Yawning at Tigers*, 20–21.

were made for. We need a God who is infinitely beautiful, but we also need one who is ultimately dangerous.

Even though we will never know God in all his infinite fullness, we were made for eternity, and the goal of eternity is to grow deeper and deeper in our relationship with this infinite, loving, dangerous God. That relationship is what we were made for and is what will most fulfill us. When God said, "You cannot see my face, for no one may see me and live" (Exodus 33:20), he was not pushing us away but was letting us know that he is infinite and that we will never tire of pursuing the depths of his infinite being for all eternity.

Fear Is a Joy That Is More Intense than Love

Nineteenth-century hymn writer Frederick William Faber wrote a poem titled "The Fear of God" that captures the relationship well between the love of God and the fear of God. Here are a few lines from the poem:

> But fear is love and love is fear,
> And in and out they move;
> But fear is an intenser joy
> Than mere unfrightened love.
>
> They love Thee little, if at all,
> Who do not fear Thee much;
> If love is Thine attraction, Lord!
> Fear is Thy very touch.
>
> And Father! When to us in heaven
> Thou shalt Thy Face unveil,
> Then more than ever will our souls
> Before Thy goodness quail.
>
> Our blessedness will be to bear
> The sight of Thee so near,
> And thus eternal love will be
> But the ecstasy of fear.[8]

8. Faber, *Faber's Hymns*, 99–101.

We don't normally associate fear with love. Faber contends, though, that there is indeed a relationship between the two. Faber is saying that joy is what fear and love have in common—the joy of experiencing God. Now that's a new thought. Just as we don't normally associate fear with love, neither do we normally associate fear with joy. What Faber is saying is that fear is a more intense experience of joy than is love. Is that not true? Fear is not a take-it-or-leave-it experience; it demands our attention. Now think of a kind of joy that demands your attention. While love is a wonderful experience, it is not so intense that it demands or captures our attention.

Imagine that you and I are in a coffee shop engrossed in a stimulating conversation. Suddenly, a gunman walks in. No matter how interesting our conversation might be, our attention would be captured by the gunman, the object of our fear. The danger the gunman presents would demand our attention. Now try to convert that evil danger into a dangerous splendor, a beauty that is dangerous, a beauty that is healthy and fulfilling, and would cause us to come alive. Then you can begin to understand how the fear of God is a more intense experience than is the love of God. While we certainly need and crave love, it is not as intense an experience as is fear. Love can be suppressed; fear can't. The experience of fear sears itself into our minds. As Faber writes, while we are attracted to God because of his love, that love becomes even more real when we fear him. If love is the experience of joy when looking at the beauty of God, fear is the experience of actually being touched by God ("If love is Thine attraction, Lord! / Fear is Thy very touch"). And when we see the unveiled face of God in heaven, we will tremble before his glory, which is when our experience of the eternal love of God will be met with "the ecstasy of fear."

The Value of Being Single-Minded

How does both fearing God and loving him make us come alive? It does so by producing in us a single-minded focus on God. David, the king of Israel, wrote, "Give me an undivided heart, / that I may fear your name" (Psalm 86:11). God told the prophet Jeremiah, "I will give them singleness of heart and action, so that they will always fear me and that all will then go well for them and for their children after them" (Jeremiah 32:39). Jesus talks about the same single-mindedness when he says that we are to "love the Lord your God with all your heart and with all your soul and with all your mind and with all your strength" (Mark 12:30). He's saying

UNDIVIDED ATTENTION: COME ALIVE BY FOCUSING ON GOD

that we should love God with all that we are. The prophet Samuel gave the following charge to the Israelites: "Be sure to fear the Lord and serve him faithfully with all your heart" (1 Samuel 12:24). Everything about us should be devoted to loving God. Nothing in us should be held back from loving him. It might come across as paradoxical, but that is the kind of love for God that the fear of God produces.

Does that kind of single-minded focus on God characterize our lives? Or is our relationship with God an experience that can be easily dismissed? Only when we have a single-minded focus on God will we come alive because we are then reflecting who we are in our true selves. Having a single-minded focus on God is who we were made to be. Many of us think that we will be most fulfilled by looking within and finding our true selves. But the exact opposite is true. Our greatest fulfillment comes when we turn our attention outside ourselves and focus it on the God who is to be feared.

Why do we need such single-mindedness? What value does it bring to our lives? How will it help us live a fulfilled life? John Piper gives a fascinating explanation of how Augustine viewed the value of having a single-minded focus on God: "For Augustine freedom is to be so much in love with God and his ways that the very experience of choice is transcended. The idea of freedom is not the autonomous will poised with sovereign equilibrium between good and evil. The idea of freedom is to be so spiritually discerning of God's beauty, and to be so in love with God that one never stands with equilibrium between God and an alternate choice. Rather, one transcends the experience of choice and walks under the continual sway of sovereign joy in God."[9] What Piper is saying through Augustine is that our love for God should cause us to be so enamored with and captivated by God's beauty, which is what the fear of God produces, that the temptation to find our fulfillment in something less than God would not even be a consideration. We should be so in love with God that the temptation of worshiping something else would be unthinkable. Why would I even consider loving something less than God? Such an idea would be laughable. We couldn't even imagine following such a temptation. Choosing to focus on something less than the overwhelming God would be choosing something less than complete and total fulfillment.

Let me illustrate what I mean through the example of fidelity in marriage. I should be so in love with my wife, so enraptured with her beauty and her personality, that the idea of even looking at another woman with

---

9. Piper, *Legacy of Sovereign Joy*, 62.

lust wouldn't even cross my mind. Indeed, it would be laughable. That single-minded devotion is what fearing God and loving him, as they work in tandem with each other, should produce in our lives.

Living with a single-minded love for God gives us true freedom. We usually think of freedom as having the ability to choose between two or more options. True freedom, though, is to be so enamored with our love for God that choosing to be enamored with something less than God is rendered unthinkable. It would be unthinkable because we realize that there is no greater beauty than that found in God. As Piper wrote, "One transcends the experience of choice and walks under the continual sway of sovereign joy in God." That is exactly what fearing God is all about! Being enthralled with God is what will make us come alive.

Is Undivided Attention Possible?

How is giving God our undivided attention even possible? After all, I can't drive and give God my undivided attention at the same time. I need to keep my attention on what I'm doing and my eyes on the road. Yes, that's true, but what I'm talking about is the inner attitude of the heart. That inner attitude might not be the most immediate thought occupying my mind, but it is still a thought that should be present to me nonetheless. Such a thought is the deep awareness of the presence of God, of being thankful to God, and of being in inner communication with God at all times.

American author Ray Bradbury said this: "There's no use having a universe, a cosmology, if you don't have witnesses. We are the witnesses to the miracle. We are put here by creation, by God. . . . We're here to be the audience to the magnificent. It is our job to celebrate."[10] Giving thanks to God for his creation is a form of that celebration that Bradbury is talking about. We often think that when we thank someone for a kindness they've shown to us, it's not much more than a throwaway line. We say thanks so automatically and with so little thought. At the same time, though, if we do something kind for someone and they don't at least say thanks, we notice it. It feels rude. How much more rude is it when we fail to give thanks to our Creator. In the book of Romans, Paul writes about those who "suppress the truth" (Romans 1:18) that God is their Creator: "For although they knew God, they neither glorified him as God nor gave thanks to him" (Romans 1:21). That passage is saying that when we fail to give thanks to God for

---

10. Bradbury, "Up Side," 9.

The Monk Who Practiced God's Presence

One of the greatest examples of someone who lived a life of giving his undivided attention to God was a monk named Brother Lawrence. His secret to giving his undivided attention to God was the realization that God is constantly present with us. Because he is present with us, we can converse with him throughout the day and night. Brother Lawrence said, "I still believe that all spiritual life consists of practicing God's presence and that anyone who practices it correctly will soon attain spiritual fulfillment."[11] His biographer wrote, "Brother Lawrence insisted that, to be constantly aware of God's presence, it is necessary to form the habit of continually talking with him throughout each day. To think that we must abandon conversation with him in order to deal with the world is erroneous."[12] Brother Lawrence is saying that, no matter what we're doing throughout the day, we're to remain in constant conversation with the God who is always present and always listening to us. That is what it means to give God our undivided attention.

The practice of giving God our undivided attention can be assisted by the first aspect of what it looks like to fear God—utter dependence. Utter dependence is a powerful emotion. Imagine being a scuba diver. The acronym SCUBA stands for Self-Contained Underwater Breathing Apparatus. As such, the entire focus of the activity of exploring underwater is focused on breathing. Why? Because that is what sustains your life when you're in the element of water. When you're exploring the wonders of the ocean, you are utterly dependent on your scuba gear. Without it, you would die. Even as you're enthralled with the beauty of the colorful fish swimming by you, or with the immensity of the whale a few feet away, or with the danger of the shark lurking yards away, your mind is never far away from thinking about that breathing apparatus. Why? Because you are utterly dependent on it. That's how we should think about God. Because we are utterly dependent on the one and only sustaining God for every breath that we take, a portion of our thinking, of our consciousness, should be focused on him, giving him our undivided attention.

---

being our Creator, we're not just being rude, we're deliberately suppressing the truth not only of who God is but also of who we are.

11. Brother Lawrence, *Practice*, "Second Letter."
12. Brother Lawrence, *Practice*, "First Conversation."

PART II: *DISCOVERING ONE'S TRUE SELF*

It says in Genesis that God "breathed the breath of life into the man's nostrils, and the man became a living person" (Genesis 2:7). With every breath that we take, then, we should be reminded that God is the one who sustains us.[13]

Being Fulfilled Through Single-Minded Devotion

Allen Levi is a singer and songwriter whose brother Gary was dying because of a brain tumor. In his book *The Last Sweet Mile: A Journey of Brothers*, Allen recounted how during the year he devoted to caring for his dying brother, he actually found himself to be the most fulfilled he had ever been. He explains, "For the first time in a long time, maybe the first time ever, my life was about one thing only: how I would serve and care for my brother, how I might embody the love of God to this one saint, each hour, every day."[14] Allen continues,

> I tell people, to their obvious surprise, that the year you [Gary] and I shared with cancer was the best year of my life. Difficult and hurtful, yes. But by any measure that really matters—depth of purpose, intensity of focus, freedom from triviality, honesty of affection, genuineness of love and joy and peace, reliance on and trust in God—it was "The Year" for me. To be with my favorite person every day, to relive so much shared history, and to be free from the petty cares that so often clutter my life added up to something for which I can find no words. I wish, of course, that I'd never experienced it, especially knowing how difficult it was for you, but I'm grateful.
>
> And in recalling it today—that last sweet mile with its uninvited joy and unexpected grace—I do so with a prayer that God will keep me at the place where I was when every day was about one thing—loving the weak (you) and trusting the strong (Him).[15]

Allen's list of why the year he spent devoted solely to taking care of his brother was so meaningful is worth repeating: "Depth of purpose, intensity of focus, freedom from triviality, honesty of affection, genuineness of love and joy and peace, reliance on and trust in God." During that year

---

13. Thanks to Pastor Chris Hodge for this thought given in a sermon on Mar. 30, 2025, at the Village Seven Presbyterian Church in Colorado Springs, CO.
14. Levi, *Last Sweet Mile*, "Unheroic."
15. Levi, *Last Sweet Mile*, "Anniversary."

of devoting himself entirely to taking care of his brother, Allen's purpose in life was clear. He was not struggling with his identity. He knew who he was, and it was founded in his purpose—to take care of his brother. When we focus on others, our identity and purpose are clear. The same holds true when we give God our undivided attention. We know who we are and what our purpose is. It is to glorify the God who is to be feared above all else. When we glorify him, we come alive and know who we are in our true selves as beings made in the image of God.

The meaning Allen found in his year of devotion to his brother is a perfect picture of the benefits we receive when giving God our undivided attention. By living for God, our purpose and identity are clear. Our identity and purpose are grounded in him who, because he is our Creator, is the only adequate foundation for who we are. When we devote ourselves to praising and thanking God with all our hearts and minds, questions about who I am and what my purpose is fall away.

Fearing God Means God's Love Demands Our Attention

Victor Frankl was a prisoner in a German concentration camp during World War II. He had lost everything—his career, his home, his family, his wife. What kept him going? Why did he survive the hopelessness of the camp when other prisoners didn't? He speaks of why he survived in his book *Man's Search for Meaning*. The context of the following story is that of Frankl and his fellow prisoners taking a long and difficult march to a work project. The inmates had been in prison for several years at this point. Their clothes were ragged and, as a result, provided no protection against the cold. They were extremely weak from having received minimal nourishment and from having to do hard labor. Frankl wrote,

> Occasionally, I looked at the sky, where the stars were fading and the pink light of the morning was beginning to spread behind a dark bank of clouds. But my mind clung to my wife's image, imagining it with an uncanny acuteness. I heard her answering me, saw her smile, her frank and encouraging look. Real or not, her look was then more luminous than the sun which was beginning to rise.
>
> A thought transfixed me: for the first time in my life I saw the truth as it is set into song by so many poets, proclaimed as the final wisdom by so many thinkers. The truth—that love is the ultimate and the highest goal to which man can aspire. Then I grasped the meaning of the greatest secret that human poetry and human

> thought and belief have to impart: *The salvation of man is through love and in love.* I understood how a man who has nothing left in this world still may know bliss, be it only for a brief moment, in the contemplation of his beloved.... For the first time in my life I was able to understand the meaning of the words, "The angels are lost in perpetual contemplation of an infinite glory."[16]

"The angels are lost in perpetual contemplation of an infinite glory." Why? Because they are enthralled and overwhelmed by the infinite glory of God. Because the beauty and the love of God compel them to give God their undivided attention. Because they are most fulfilled when gazing at the glory of God.

It is in being "lost in perpetual contemplation of an infinite glory" that the fear of God and the love of God merge. What does fear do? It takes our focus off ourselves and demands that we focus on the object of fear. What does love do? It fulfills us. It makes us come alive. It completes us. It makes us know what we were made for. While fear demands our undivided attention, the "demand" of fearing God does not mean we are forced against our will to look at God. Instead, the "demand" produced by the fear of God is the fulfilling compulsion that love produces in our lives to gaze at the absolute beauty and incomprehensible love of God. To fear God means we are so enthralled with the unbelievable beauty and infinite love of God that turning away from looking at him, and instead looking at ourselves, would be unthinkable. It would be unthinkable because choosing to focus on ourselves instead of on God would be like choosing to gaze at a dim candle rather than at a brilliant sunrise shining in all its glory. It would be settling for so much less than what we were meant to experience.

Questions for Personal Reflection or Group Discussion

1. How is the danger of God related to our being fulfilled in him?
2. How is fearing God related to loving God?
3. Why does fearing God make us come alive?

---

16. Frankl, *Man's Search for Meaning*, 56–57.

UNDIVIDED ATTENTION: COME ALIVE BY FOCUSING ON GOD

4. How does the analogy of the scuba diver help you understand what it means to live with undivided attention toward God?

5. How did the story of Allen Levi's devotion to his brother Gary affect you?

6

Unshakable Trust: Trusting in the Goodness of the God Who Cares

IF ANYONE HAD CAUSE to question God's goodness and trustworthiness, it was Abraham, the first patriarch of the Jews. Why? Because God seemed to go against his own word. He had promised one thing to Abraham, and then it appeared that he was removing the means by which that promise could be fulfilled.

Here's the situation. God had made a promise to Abraham: "I will make you very fruitful; I will make nations of you, and kings will come from you" (Genesis 17:6). There was a serious obstacle, though, when it came to fulfilling that promise. Abraham and Sarah had no son through whom the promise could be fulfilled. The passage in the book of Genesis says that Abraham fell facedown when he received these words of promise, but inwardly "he laughed and said to himself, 'Will a son be born to a man a hundred years old? Will Sarah bear a child at the age of ninety?'" (Genesis 17:17). God did not withdraw his promise, though. He instead responded by saying, "Yes, but your wife Sarah will bear you a son, and you will call him Isaac. I will establish my covenant with him as an everlasting covenant for his descendants after him" (Genesis 17:19). It was indeed a miracle that Isaac was born to Abraham and Sarah.

When God's Words Don't Make Sense

But then the unthinkable happened, which is why Abraham had good reason to question God's goodness and trustworthiness. When Isaac was a young man, God spoke again to Abraham and, without explanation, commanded Abraham to sacrifice Isaac: "Take your son, your only son, whom you love—Isaac—and go to the region of Moriah. Sacrifice him there as a burnt offering on a mountain I will show you" (Genesis 22:2). How could God command such a thing? After all, Isaac was the son through whom he was to fulfill the promise he had made to Abraham. How could he then command Abraham to kill him? What kind of God is this anyway? Is he not good? Is he not trustworthy?

How do you see God? Do you see him as someone who can't be trusted, who goes back on his word, who will only disappoint you, whose only goal is to take from you what is most precious to you? Do you see God as someone who wants to take from you whatever gives you the most joy?

The story of Abraham and Isaac continues:

> Early the next morning Abraham got up and loaded his donkey. He took with him two of his servants and his son Isaac. When he had cut enough wood for the burnt offering, he set out for the place God had told him about. On the third day Abraham looked up and saw the place in the distance. He said to his servants, "Stay here with the donkey while I and the boy go over there. We will worship and then we will come back to you."
>
> Abraham took the wood for the burnt offering and placed it on his son Isaac, and he himself carried the fire and the knife. As the two of them went on together, Isaac spoke up and said to his father Abraham, "Father?"
>
> "Yes, my son?" Abraham replied.
>
> "The fire and wood are here," Isaac said, "but where is the lamb for the burnt offering?"
>
> Abraham answered, "God himself will provide the lamb for the burnt offering, my son." And the two of them went on together. (Genesis 22:3–8)

Why did Abraham obey God by doing the unthinkable—almost killing his own son? Was it out of sheer terror of God? Was it because God is the kind of God who needs to be appeased with human sacrifice, as was a common practice in the surrounding cultures? Was it because Abraham was more afraid of God than he was of sacrificing his own son, as terrible as that was? Did he see God as a tyrant who expected him to do the unthinkable so as to put Abraham in his place? That's how it appears. Abraham's obedience is hard for us to understand.

Abraham, though, viewed God very differently from the way in which many of us view God. Abraham had an astonishing amount of trust in the goodness and the trustworthiness of God. Even when God's words didn't make sense, Abraham still trusted him.

We see evidence of Abraham's unshakable trust in God's goodness and trustworthiness in two places in the biblical passage. The first is in verse 5. After walking for three days and seeing the mountain in the distance where the sacrifice was to take place, Abraham told his servants to stay where they were while he and Isaac went to the top of the mountain to make the sacrifice. He then said, "*We* will worship and then *we* will come back to you" (Genesis 22:5, emphasis added). Abraham used the term "we," not "I." If Abraham was intending to obey God by sacrificing Isaac, how could he say that they would both return to the servants? Was Abraham purposely deceiving his servants because of the unthinkable nature of what he was about to do, or did he truly believe that both he and Isaac would be returning to them? It's very possible that he truly believed they would both be returning. Why do I say that? Because of the second piece of evidence found in verses 7–8.

The second piece of evidence that Abraham trusted in God's goodness is found in the way he answered his son when Isaac observed that they had the wood and the fire for the sacrifice but not the animal: "Where is the lamb for the burnt offering?" (Genesis 22:7). Abraham answered, "God himself will provide the lamb for the burnt offering, my son" (Genesis 22:8). He had no idea how God would provide, but he trusted that God would indeed provide.

It's hard to imagine a scene that could contain more dramatic tension than the scene of Abraham who, after putting his son on the altar and out of unquestioning obedience to God, raised his hand and was about to plunge the knife into the heart of his own son. His mind must have been filled with questions. "Why did God provide the miracle of a son born to Sarah and me in our old age, only to now have me kill him? Why would God make the promise of many nations coming from me through my son Isaac only to then command that I kill him? What God has commanded me to do doesn't make any sense. Why am I doing this? I know that God is good and that he is trustworthy, but I don't understand!" Then, at the very moment Abraham was about to plunge the knife into Isaac, God said, "Do not lay a hand on the boy. . . . Do not do anything to him" (Genesis 22:12). At that very moment, a ram appeared in the thicket that God had provided for Abraham to sacrifice in the place of Isaac.

Why did God put Abraham through such a terrible test of faith? Here's why: "Now I know that you fear God, because you have not withheld from me your son, your only son" (Genesis 22:12). It was all about whether Abraham feared God. What did that mean? What was God looking for from Abraham?

First, he was looking for whether Abraham feared, or worshiped, God above all else, including his son Isaac. To worship God above all else because he alone is God is what it means to fear God. It would have been so easy for Abraham to make Isaac the be-all and end-all of his life. After all, he was a clear gift from God, and he was the means by which God was going to bless Abraham. God knew how much Isaac meant to Abraham. When he commanded Abraham to sacrifice Isaac, he referred to Isaac as "your son, your only son, Isaac, whom you love" (Genesis 22:2). Considering how much Isaac meant to Abraham, it would have been understandable if Abraham had raised the level of his relationship with Isaac to be more important to him than his relationship with God. When God commanded Abraham to sacrifice Isaac, he could have responded by saying, "No, he's mine." By doing so, he would have pitted himself against God. But Abraham realized Isaac was not his. Because Abraham obeyed God and was willing to give up his only son, the son he loved, at God's request, God said, "I swear by myself, declares the Lord, that because you have done this and have not withheld your son, your only son, I will surely bless you and make your descendants as numerous as the stars in the sky and as the sand on the seashore" (Genesis 22:16–17).

Second, God was looking for whether Abraham trusted him even when things didn't make sense. He was looking to see if Abraham saw God as being good and trustworthy. The author of the book of Hebrews gives his Holy Spirit–inspired explanation as to why Abraham obeyed God when he had commanded him to sacrifice his son: "By faith Abraham, when God tested him, offered Isaac as a sacrifice. He who had embraced the promises was about to sacrifice his one and only son, even though God had said to him, 'It is through Isaac that your offspring will be reckoned.' Abraham reasoned that God could even raise the dead, and so in a manner of speaking he did receive Isaac back from death" (Hebrews 11:17–19).

What are these verses implying? They're implying that Abraham realized his utter dependence on God. Because God was the Creator of all things, he had the power to give life back to the son he had commanded Abraham to sacrifice. Because Abraham was utterly dependent on God, he could trust in God's goodness, and he knew that God could be trusted to somehow keep his promise even though he had no idea how.

Here we see the theme of utter dependence come up again in our discussion of what fearing God looks like. We saw it before when talking about giving God our undivided attention. I had written that because we are utterly dependent on the one and only sustaining God for every breath that we take, a portion of our thinking, of our consciousness, should be focused on him, giving him our undivided attention. And now we see that utter dependence come up again in regard to Abraham having an unshakable trust in God. He knew that God, as the Creator of all things, had the power to raise Isaac from the dead, and so he could then trust God to accomplish his promise. Abraham realized that he was utterly dependent on him who had the power to create all things, and that utter dependence was transferred into unshakable trust because he knew that if God had the power to create, he also had the power to provide by raising Isaac from the dead.

The God Who Is Above the Storm

There is a story in the Bible that, like the story of Abraham, talks about having faith in God even when experiences in life don't make sense. It's the story where Jesus calms the storm:

> That day when evening came, he said to his disciples, "Let us go over to the other side." Leaving the crowd behind, they took him along, just as he was, in the boat. There were also other boats with him. A furious squall came up, and the waves broke over the boat, so that it was nearly swamped. Jesus was in the stern, sleeping on a cushion. The disciples woke him and said to him, "Teacher, don't you care if we drown?"
>
> He got up, rebuked the wind and said to the waves, "Quiet! Be still!" Then the wind died down and it was completely calm.
>
> He said to his disciples, "Why are you so afraid? Do you still have no faith?"
>
> They were terrified and asked each other, "Who is this? Even the wind and the waves obey him!" (Mark 4:35–41)

After Jesus rebuked the wind and quieted the waves, he then turned to his disciples and asked them, "Why are you so afraid? Do you still have no faith?" I honestly can't relate to Jesus at this point. If I were one of his disciples I would have said, "What do you mean, 'Why were we afraid,' Jesus? We were about to drown! The water was filling the boat so that it was about to sink! Couldn't you see that, Jesus?" I can relate much more to the fear of the disciples. It seems that Jesus is being unreasonable in what he was expecting from the disciples. Since this story happened toward the beginning of Jesus' ministry when he hadn't done that many miracles, Jesus certainly couldn't have expected his disciples to think he had the power to control the overwhelming forces of nature.

Plus, this experience of almost dying by drowning just didn't make sense. The disciples didn't yet have a full-fledged understanding of who Jesus was, but they knew there was something special about him. They believed that God's hand was on Jesus in a unique way. That's why they chose to follow him and to devote their lives to him. Here, though, they were about to die a meaningless death in the middle of the night in the middle of the sea. It just didn't make sense.

What, then, was Jesus attempting to teach his disciples with his questions, "Why are you so afraid? Do you still have no faith?" Remember that Jesus was dealing with people who had grown up hearing the stories of the Old Testament, the stories of how God had miraculously delivered the Israelites from their slavery to the Egyptians with the ten plagues and of how, as the Egyptian army pursued the Israelites, God had parted the waters of the Red Sea so the Israelites could walk through it. These were stories that showed God's power over nature and how God cared for his people. With his questions, "Why are you so afraid? Do you still have no faith?" Jesus was helping them see that they were making the storm ultimate and were forgetting that God is the one who is ultimate over the storm. To fear God is to live in the context of a God who is above the storms of life. Fearing God is all about context. What is the ultimate context in which we live our lives? Is it our troubles, or is it God?

King David knew what it meant to live in the context of a God who is to be feared above all else: "The LORD is my light and my salvation— / whom shall I fear? / The LORD is the stronghold of my life— / of whom shall I be afraid?" (Psalm 27:1). Also, God told the people of Israel, "So do not fear, for I am with you; do not be dismayed, for I am your God. I will strengthen you and help you; I will uphold you with my righteous right hand" (Isaiah 41:10). That promise can be applied to God's people today as well.

The Importance of Context

Let me illustrate the importance of context in this way. The Space Shuttle *Challenger* was amazing in that it had an enormous amount of power packed into it. The fuel used to propel the shuttle away from the strong pull of the earth's gravity was contained in the external tank and the two solid rocket boosters. The external tank contained 143,351 gallons of liquid oxygen and 385,265 gallons of liquid hydrogen, which were combined to power the shuttle's engines. The two boosters contained over 1.1 million pounds of solid fuel. Once that fuel was ignited, there was no stopping the burn until all the fuel was expended.[1]

The NASA personnel who prepared and monitored the launch of the shuttle could not have been more careful and cautious. Still, even with all the precautions taken, tragedy struck on January 28, 1986. As the *Challenger* lifted off, everything appeared to be normal until, seventy-three seconds into its flight, the *Challenger* exploded into an orange and white fireball, tragically killing all seven crew members on board.

Jay Green, the shuttle's flight director in Houston, said, "When you have that much power you have to respect it. If you get complacent about the launch phase, you don't understand what's going on."[2] Mr. Green's comment had to do with context. He was saying that when the kind of power contained in the shuttle's rockets is being harnessed, one should always be mindful of it. It should be a part of one's thinking constantly, and it should never be taken lightly.

Do we understand what's going on? Are we aware of the ultimate context in which we live? Could it be that we are oblivious to the fact that we live in the context of the God who is infinitely more powerful than even the millions of pounds of fuel contained in the *Challenger*?

To fear God means to live in the context of an all-powerful and absolutely good God so that we have an unshakable faith and trust in him. The psalmist wrote, "You who fear him, trust in the LORD— / he is their help and shield" (Psalm 115:11). If we fear God, we should not be afraid of anything else. English professor Grant Horner writes, "Paradoxically, the

---

1. Magnuson, "They Slipped the Surly Bonds," 27
2. Magnuson, "They Slipped the Surly Bonds," 27

God who is worthy of fear promises those who trust in him that they do not need to be afraid of him in the normal fallen sense. God's words of comfort to Abraham in Genesis 15:1 are typical: 'Fear not, Abram [God changed his name to Abraham later], I am your shield . . .' There is a marvelous irony here. The one thing in the universe we really should fear—God—protects us from himself by enacting his grace for our benefit and his glory. Thus, if you fear him you have no need to be afraid. If you do not fear him you have every reason to be afraid."[3]

In his book *Yawning at Tigers*, Drew Dyck defines the fear of God in this way: "To fear the Lord is to be grounded in reality, to have an accurate view of God's holy nature and of his awesome power."[4] Fearing God puts everything else in its proper perspective; it's "to be grounded in reality," and that reality is that God is to be feared above all else because he is above all things, and that should comfort us when we encounter storms in our life.

Holding Onto

Consider this dialogue between Frodo and Sam in *The Lord of the Rings: The Two Towers*:

> FRODO. I can't do this, Sam.
>
> SAM. I know. It's all wrong. By rights we shouldn't even be here. But we are. It's like in the great stories, Mr. Frodo. The ones that really mattered. Full of darkness and danger, they were. And sometimes you didn't want to know the end. Because how could the end be happy? How could the world go back to the way it was when so much bad had happened? But in the end, it's only a passing thing, this shadow. Even darkness must pass. A new day will come. And when the sun shines it will shine out the clearer. Those were the stories that stayed with you. That meant something, even if you were too small to understand why. But think, Mr. Frodo, I do understand. I know now. Folk in those stories had lots of chances of turning back, only they didn't. They kept going. Because they were holding on to something.
>
> FRODO. What are we holding onto, Sam?

---

3. Horner, *Meaning at the Movies*, 131.
4. Dyck, *Yawning at Tigers*, 59.

SAM. That there's some good in this world, Mr. Frodo, and it's worth fighting for.[5]

If I may be so presumptuous, I want to adjust Sam's answer to Frodo's question where he asked, "What are we holding onto?" I want to adjust it to, "*Who* are we holding onto?" In the face of the darkness where suffering seems to make no sense, we should hold onto the goodness and the trustworthiness of God. Why? Because the God who is good is the foundation for all that we know to be good in the world. There is good in the world only because God, the Creator of the world and the absolute standard of goodness, is good. Who, not what, should we hold onto? We should hold onto the God who is absolute in his goodness and who is therefore the foundation for goodness in the world. Our only hope is to hold tightly onto that good God who cares for us.

I like the term that Sam used: "holding onto." I like it because it conveys the sense of desperation and the fact that we have no hope in ourselves. It conveys the knowledge that God is our only hope. That is exactly what it means to fear God and to be utterly dependent on him. To "hold onto" God is to put all the suffering and evil in the world in the proper context of the God who is good and trustworthy and who has ultimate power over the turmoil and troubles of the world. The psalmist writes, "How abundant are the good things / that you have stored up for those who fear you, / which you bestow in the sight of all, / on those who take refuge in you" (Psalm 31:19). To "take refuge" in God is another way of saying "hold onto."

Continuing to Trust God Through Trials

The story of Yosely Pereira's escape from Castro's Cuba is a captivating example of trusting in God in the midst of terrible persecution and suffering. Yosely did not always believe in God. In fact, he had hoped that there was no god because he had seen what he thought god was like. Growing up in Cuba, he had been indoctrinated even in elementary school into believing that Castro was god. But because this "god" and his minions persecuted and publicly humiliated Yosely and his family, they knew he had to escape from Castro's tyrannical regime. Yosely's views about God changed, however, in the most unlikely of places—in prison.

---

5. Jackson, *Two Towers*, 2:44:32.

Castro had declared that all able-bodied young men older than sixteen were required to serve three years in the Cuban Revolutionary Armed Forces. Yosely didn't know how he could possibly do that because he was the primary breadwinner for his family, which consisted of his mother and sister. They would starve without him. So he hid from the authorities. In the middle of one night, though, there was a loud knock on their door. Three soldiers barged in, arrested Yosely, and took him to prison. While in the prison yard, he noticed another prisoner pull something out from a small bush. Yosely feared that it might be a weapon. After a few nights, the prisoner saw Yosely looking at him and asked, "You want to know what is in the bush?" Yosely, scared, answered, "No." On the next night Yosely saw this man pull out the object from the bush again. This time, though, the man asked Yosely, "Can you read?" Yosely nodded, "Yes." Then the man gave him a book, saying, "Hold on to this. It will protect you." Yosely quickly tucked it into the belt of his pants because to be caught with any kind of contraband would mean torture and perhaps even death.[6]

The task Yosely and the other prisoners were given was to work twelve- to sixteen-hour days harvesting agave plants. The thorns of the agave plant are extremely sharp. Because a thorn had become lodged in Yosely's left foot, he developed a fever and his foot became infected, swelling to twice its normal size. After threatening to cut his foot off if it didn't get better, the guards gave him three days off from work so his foot would heal. This reprieve gave him a chance to read the book he had been given, which was a Bible. He randomly opened it and just happened to read Isaiah 41:10: "Do not fear, for I am with you; do not be dismayed, for I am your God. I will strengthen you and help you; I will uphold you with my righteous right hand." After reading those words over and over again, Yosely remembers that he "wept uncontrollably for what seemed like hours as those words echoed in my head. For the first time in my life, I saw the goodness of what a true God should be. *A protector and a provider. A God who is with me and who will never leave.*"[7] Almost four months later, Yosely "hobbled home with that tiny book tucked into the waistband of [his] jeans—more determined than ever to get out of Cuba."[8]

In preparation for his escape from Cuba, Yosely would sneak away from home at night when his family was sleeping to build a 12 × 5 × 3½

---

6. Pereira and Ivey, *Sea Between Us*, "I Am with You."
7. Pereira and Ivey, *Sea Between Us*, "I Am with You"; emphasis in original.
8. Pereira and Ivey, *Sea Between Us*, "I Am with You."

foot boat by hand. On February 7, the night Yosely and his four friends had chosen to escape, Yosely snuck away from home without telling his wife so that she would honestly not know where her husband was when the police came asking. After two and a half days of rowing, their hands were blistered, they were sunburned from exposure to the unrelenting sun, the vast ocean was all they could see in every direction, and they were without water and without food because their bag of food had floated away during a violent storm. Thinking of the passage from Isaiah, Yosely started whispering to himself, "I am with you." Each time he said it, his voice grew more loud. Eventually Alberto, a friend in the boat, asked him,

"Are you okay, Yosely?"

"Do you believe in God?" [asked Yosely.]

"Which one?" Alberto said, laughing. "The only god I have ever known is Fidel. Do I believe in him? Yes. Unfortunately, he is very real."

"You know what I mean. The God from the Bible."

"I don't know," [Alberto] replied honestly. "I haven't read it, and I don't know anything about Him. But if He can save us," he said with a smile, "I will certainly believe anything you want, Yosely."

[Alberto] paused thoughtfully. "Do you believe in Him?"

[Yosely] looked up and met Alberto's eyes. "I used to. I used to think He was watching us, protecting us. But I don't know anymore."

[Yosely] sat up, inched closer, and whispered, "I don't know if we are going to make it . . ."

At that precise moment, a massive storm cloud covered the sun and a dark calm covered us. [Yosely] felt a raindrop. Then another . . .

Is this really happening? [Yosely thought.]

"I was thirsty and you gave me drink" [Yosely] said, laughing and nodding to [himself]. Looking up, [he] shouted, "I am with you!"[9]

Amazingly, Yosely and three of his four friends (one died along the way) made it to Florida. God provided people to help Yosely each step of the way, including an American who continued to hire him day after day so Yosely could make the money needed to live and to rescue Yosely's wife, Taire, and their two children from Cuba. While there were two unsuccessful

9. Pereira and Ivey, *Sea Between Us*, "I Am with You"; emphasis in original.

attempts to free his family from Cuba, Yosely, after two long and difficult years, was finally reunited with his family. During that time of waiting, Yosely was often reminded of the verse in Isaiah where God promised to be with him. Yosely wrote, "Maybe that's what God was trying to say when He promised to always be with me. Maybe He was working through all the people—all the ups and downs throughout my life—to bring me here to this point. To my family."[10]

As with Yosely, the troubles of life can cause our faith in the presence, the goodness, and the trustworthiness of God to be tested and even shaken. In the end, though, the truth of Isaiah 41:10 never changes: "Do not fear, for I am with you; do not be dismayed, for I am your God. I will strengthen you and help you; I will uphold you with my righteous right hand." To fear God is to desperately hold onto, to cling to, that truth.

Trusting in God's Goodness

The monk Brother Lawrence (mentioned earlier) lived with a "confidence in God's goodness [that] made him certain that he would never leave him entirely."[11] He believed that we "have a God who is infinitely good and who knows what he is doing. He will come to deliver you from your present trouble in his perfect time and when you may least expect it. Hope in Him more than ever."[12] His biographer wrote,

> Faith gave Brother Lawrence a firm hope in God's goodness, confidence in His providence, and the ability to completely abandon himself into God's hands. He never worried about what would become of him; rather, he threw himself into the arms of infinite mercy. The more desperate things appeared to him, the more he hoped—like a rock beaten by the waves of the sea and yet settling itself more firmly in the midst of the tempest. This is why he said that the greatest glory one can give to God is to entirely mistrust one's own strength, relying completely on God's protection. This constitutes a sincere recognition of one's weakness and a true confession of the omnipotence of the Creator.[13]

---

10. Pereira and Ivey, *Sea Between Us*, "Esta Es America."
11. Lawrence, *Practice*, "Third Conversation."
12. Lawrence, *Practice*, "Seventh Letter."
13. Joseph Beaufort, as quoted in Lawrence, *Practice*, part 4.

Brother Lawrence knew what it meant to fear God and to be utterly dependent on God, which caused him to have an unshakable trust in God.

Allen Levi, who devoted his life to taking care of his dying brother, also wrote of having an unshakable trust in the goodness of God: "We did not lose faith, ever, in the possibility that God might heal Gary of cancer, either miraculously or medically. We never gave up that hope. But we did surrender. Not to the disease, but to God. We would trust Him. . . . We resigned ourselves to the goodness of God."[14]

God and Conspiracy Theories

The prophet Isaiah gives us perspective concerning what it means to fear God amid a troubled world: "Do not call conspiracy everything that these people call conspiracy; do not fear what they fear. . . . The LORD Almighty is the one you are to regard as holy, he is the one you are to fear" (Isaiah 8:12–13). There are many things in this world that cause us to be anxious and worried; they are too numerous to count. Conspiracy theories are one of them. Conspiracy theories represent the fear of something hidden, secretive, and unknown that is outside our control. And yet Isaiah exhorts us to fear God above all else, even conspiracy theories. Why? Because God has power over all things and is also sovereign over all of history.

What happens, then, when we fear such an almighty God? Here is where this passage in Isaiah gets interesting because it takes a turn that is unexpected. Isaiah begins by saying that we are to fear God, but then he completes that thought by saying, "And he will be a holy place [or sanctuary]" (Isaiah 8:14a). Isaiah goes from telling us that we are to fear this almighty, all-powerful God to then saying that when we fear him, we will find him to be our sanctuary. A sanctuary is a place of rest, peace, and safety. Isaiah is saying that we can find rest, peace, and safety in God because he is the greatest power that exists—and is therefore to be feared. The unspoken thought, though, is that we can find rest, peace, and safety in God not only because he is the greatest power that exists but also because God is good, trustworthy, and caring. God is worthy of our unshakable trust, and that unshakable trust will give us rest for our souls. As the Bible says, "Whoever fears the LORD has a secure fortress" (Proverbs 14:26).

---

14. Levi, *Last Sweet Mile*, "Call."

Questions for Personal Reflection or Group Discussion

1. What is God like to you? What is your view of God?
2. What would you have done if you had been Abraham?
3. What is the context in which you live your life? Has this chapter changed your perspective as to what your context should be? How?
4. When you face troubles or suffering, what are your thoughts about God?
5. Why can God be our sanctuary, our place of rest?

Evidence and Arguments for the God Who Is to Be Feared

7

Why Is There Something Rather than Nothing?

We've just finished talking about what it means to fear God and what the characteristics are of a person who fears God. Before we go further, though, we need to address an important question: Is there evidence that God exists, especially a God who has created all things? It doesn't make sense to talk about being made in the image of God and of fearing God if God does not exist. So, before we proceed, we will look at some of the evidence and the arguments that point to God's existence.

The purpose of this chapter is not to be exhaustive when it comes to evidence and arguments that confirm God's existence. As we saw in chapter 4 (Utter Dependence: Being Overwhelmed by Our Creator), our being utterly dependent on God for our existence is one of the three characteristics as to what it looks like to fear God. Because of that, my primary focus will be to show that God as Creator exists.

An Infinitely Old Universe Is Just as Plausible as a Creator God

Astrophysicist and atheist Carl Sagan didn't think there was a need for a Creator. Even though Sagan died in 1996, he's still a worthy representative of those who argue against the universe needing a Creator. Sagan wrote,

> First of all, it is perfectly possible that the universe is infinitely old and therefore requires no Creator. This is consistent with existing

> knowledge of cosmology, which permits an oscillating universe in which the events since the Big Bang are merely the latest incarnation in an infinite series of creations and destructions of the universe. But secondly, let us consider the idea of a universe created somehow from nothing by God. The question naturally arises—and many ten-year-olds spontaneously think of it before being discouraged by their elders—where does God come from? If we answer that God is infinitely old or present simultaneously in all epochs, we have solved nothing, except perhaps verbally. We have merely postponed by one step coming to grips with the problem. A universe that is infinitely old and a God that is infinitely old are, I think, equally deep mysteries. It is not readily apparent why one should be considered more reliably established than the other.[1]

Sagan writes that "it is perfectly possible that the universe is infinitely old," thereby dismissing the need for a Creator. Such a statement, however, is not beyond dispute. The ideas that the universe had a beginning and that it needed a Creator have not always been the consensus opinion among scientists. That consensus has changed, however. Renowned British physicist Paul Davies wrote that "today, few cosmologists doubt that the universe, as least as we know it, did have an origin at a finite moment in the past."[2] There are several points of evidence that point to the universe having a beginning, but the following two are the strongest.

First, there's the red shift of the galaxies, which indicates that the universe is expanding. To be more precise, space is not expanding into some form of preexisting emptiness, but it is "the expansion of space itself."[3] The Bible speaks of this expansion when it says, "[God] alone stretches out the heavens" (Job 9:8). The term "red shift" describes something similar to the change in sound that we experience when, as a train moves away from us, the sound of its horn goes from higher to lower in pitch. The same is happening with the light from the galaxies. Because they are moving away from us, the light waves move toward the red—or longer—end of the spectrum. The expansion of the universe, when extrapolated back, points to the planets, stars, and galaxies moving away from a singularity, which is an infinitely dense point at the beginning of time and space. Cosmologists John Barrow and Frank Tipler write, "At this singularity, space and time came into

---

1. Sagan, *Broca's Brain*, 287.
2. Copan and Craig, *Creation out of Nothing*, 244.
3. Copan and Craig, *Creation out of Nothing*, 222.

existence; literally nothing existed before the singularity, so, if the Universe originated at such a singularity, we would truly have a creation *ex nihilo*."[4]

Second, there's the evidence of the second law of thermodynamics, which says that while the total amount of energy remains constant (the first law of thermodynamics), the availability of usable energy is constantly decreasing and becoming inaccessible. The second law is what makes drinking a hot cup of coffee in the morning so frustrating because it goes from hot to lukewarm so quickly.

How is the second law of thermodynamics relevant to the beginning of the universe? As vast as the universe is, it's still finite. Plus, it's also a closed universe, which means that no new physical energy is being added to it. If the energy of the universe is finite but the universe has existed for an eternity (an infinite amount of time) with no starting point, then the finite amount of energy in the universe would have been used up by now.

Sagan accuses those who put forward the Creator hypothesis as having solved nothing, but of only having "postponed by one step coming to grips with the problem." In truth, he is even more guilty of his own accusation because with his theory of an oscillating universe, he has pushed back the problem not just one step but an infinite number of steps. That's called an infinite regression, and an infinite regression is impossible.

Let me illustrate the impossibility of an infinite regression in this way. Imagine that you want to play soccer, but you don't possess a soccer ball. So you go to your neighbor to ask to borrow a soccer ball from him. But he doesn't possess one either. So he goes to his neighbor to borrow a soccer ball. Regrettably, he doesn't possess one either. If this series goes on into infinity, then it never has a starting point, and you never come to possess a soccer ball. For you to possess a soccer ball, that series must end with someone actually possessing a soccer ball. The same is true of our existence. Since our existence is contingent, which means it is "borrowed" from something else, then that "something else" must possess existence in itself so that we could come to exist. Sagan's infinite regression of oscillating universes, however, never stops; it has no beginning point. Therefore, Sagan has no explanation for how a finite and contingent universe came to be.

The philosophical argument for the universe having a beginning and therefore needing a self-existing Creator is called the cosmological argument, which addresses the question as to why there is something rather

---

4. Copan and Craig, *Creation out of Nothing*, 222.

than nothing. The following is philosopher Gregory Ganssle's version of that argument:

> Premise 1: Whatever comes into existence is caused to exist by something else.
>
> Premise 2: If the series of past causes is not infinite, then the series of past causes came into existence.
>
> Premise 3: There cannot be an infinite series of past causes.
>
> Conclusion 1: Therefore, the series of past causes came into existence.
>
> Conclusion 2: Therefore, there exists a cause for the series of past causes, and this cause did not itself come into existence.[5]

Remember that Sagan had said that an "infinitely old" God solves nothing because "the question naturally arises—and many ten-year-olds spontaneously think of it before being discouraged by their elders—where does God come from?" Notice, though, that the cosmological argument does not begin with the statement that whatever *exists* is caused by something else. That would indeed mean that even God, who exists, would need a cause for his existence. Instead, the first premise is "Whatever *comes into existence* is caused to exist by something else" (emphasis added). God did not come into existence but has always existed and therefore doesn't need a cause for his existence.

We saw, moreover, that because an infinite regression is impossible, the best explanation for the starting point is a God who has existence within himself and was the uncaused First Cause. So the ten-year-old's question does not make sense. God was not caused by anything prior to him. God simply exists; his existence is necessary, not contingent.

Besides the Creator God having existence in himself, there are other conclusions we can draw about the nature of the Creator from the universe having a beginning and being created from nothing. Norm Geisler and Frank Turek spell out what the nature of the First Cause must be like from the fact that the space/time universe had a beginning. According to them, the First Cause must be

- self-existent, timeless, nonspatial, and immaterial (since the First Cause created time, space, and matter, the First Cause must be outside

---

5. Ganssle, *Thinking About God*, 44–45.

of time, space, and matter). In other words, he is without limits, or infinite;

- unimaginably powerful, to create the universe out of nothing;
- supremely intelligent, to design the universe with such incredible precision . . . ;
- personal, in order to choose to convert a state of nothingness into the time-space-material universe (an impersonal force has no ability to make choices).[6]

Geisler and Turek go on to write, "These characteristics of the First Cause are exactly the characteristics theists ascribe to God,"[7] and they match with how the Bible describes God.

God as Sustainer

The Bible talks about God being not only the Creator but also the Sustainer of all things: God "[sustains] all things by his powerful word" (Hebrews 1:3). For those who are not convinced that the universe had a beginning, there is also the argument that God continuously sustains the universe in its existence each moment. Dr. Robert Spitzer, a Jesuit priest, philosopher, and educator, has developed an argument coming from that perspective. He argues that creation, meaning the space/time universe, is a conditioned reality. A conditioned reality is "any reality . . . that is *dependent* upon another reality for its existence or occurrence."[8] Spitzer explains that a cat is a conditioned reality that depends on cells, and cells are a conditioned reality that depend on molecules, and molecules depend on atoms, and atoms depend on quarks.[9] How far down, though, does it go? Is there ever an end to this string of conditions? Spitzer writes that there are two possibilities when it comes to this string of conditioned realities.

First, there is the possibility of a finite string of conditions that uphold the conditioned reality of the cat. The problem with that scenario, though, is that "the last condition must be a conditioned reality whose conditions [for existence] are not fulfilled." What that means is that the last condition

---

6. Geisler and Turek, *I Don't Have Enough Faith*, 93.
7. Geisler and Turek, *I Don't Have Enough Faith*, 93.
8. Spitzer, *New Proofs*, ch. 3, §1.E; emphasis in original.
9. Spitzer, *New Proofs*, ch. 3, §1.A.

cannot exist because the conditions necessary for it to exist and to be real are not met or fulfilled.[10] Since it does not exist, it is nothing.

Second, there is the possibility of an infinite string of conditions to uphold the conditioned reality of the cat. That means that there is no "most fundamental condition" or "last condition" because an infinite string is simply not achievable. This is, as mentioned before, the impossibility of an the infinite regression. Spitzer writes that if our conditioned reality "is dependent upon a dependent upon a dependent upon a dependent, *ad infinitum*, in order to come into existence, it will never come into existence. Its conditions will never be fulfilled."[11]

The inability of the first two possibilities to explain the conditioned reality of the cat leads to the conclusion that for a conditioned reality to exist, it must be based on an unconditioned reality, which is defined as "a reality that does not depend on any other reality of any kind for its existence or occurrence."[12] That sounds a lot like the biblical definition of the God who has existence within himself, who is self-existent, and who is the uncaused Cause. Spitzer draws out the implications of this line of reasoning. He writes that while the necessity of an unconditioned reality does not rule out the one-time act of God creating the universe from nothing, it also includes the possibility that the Creator God is "continuously fulfilling conditions ultimately, and . . . 'holding or conserving' conditioned realities in being."[13] He continues, "The Creator . . . must be a *continuous* Creator . . . of all else that is real at every moment. . . . Analogously speaking, if the Creator stopped 'thinking' about us, we would literally lapse into nothingness."[14] There is, therefore, good reason to believe that for us to exist from moment to moment, God, the self-existent one, must sustain us.

Other Evidence and Arguments

There are other evidence and arguments that point to the existence of a Creator God who has personal attributes. For example, the existence of information in our DNA requires a transcendent mind as its source. Each strand of DNA contains an immense amount of information. If the code

---

10. Spitzer, *New Proofs*, ch. 3, §1.B.
11. Spitzer, *New Proofs*, ch. 3, §1.C; emphasis in original.
12. Spitzer, *New Proofs*, ch. 3, §1.E.
13. Spitzer, *New Proofs*, ch. 3, §5.B.
14. Spitzer, *New Proofs*, ch. 3, §5.B; emphasis in original.

contained in the DNA were typed on 8½ × 11 inch sheets of paper and stacked one on top of the other, the stack would reach 555 feet high, which is as tall as the Washington Monument.[15] And that's the amount of information in *each strand* of DNA. What in our experience is the source of information? Mind, not matter. What, though, can produce that amount of information? Only the mind of an infinitely intelligent God.

There's also the existence of linguistic conventions. Imagine walking on a sandy beach and encountering these words written on the beach: "Bob loves Mary." What or who would you think caused those words to appear on the beach? There are three options: the laws of nature, chance, or a person with intelligence. The laws of nature, such as the random running of the waves and the blowing of the wind, would cause regular patterns, but they would not be able to cause the irregular shapes of the letters. Chance could perhaps account for the complexity of the letters but not for the specified nature of the letters. Neither could chance account for the information contained in the letters. The best explanation for those words written on the beach is an intelligent person. Such intelligence accounts for the complexity of the letters, the specified nature of the letters, and the information contained in the letters.

There's another factor that those letters point to, and that's called the linguistic convention, which is the factor that is needed to interpret the information in the letters. What's interesting is that linguistic conventions are not tied directly to the physical code itself. How do we know this? For example, the letters s-e-e mean "sight" in English but "ocean" in German. If the meaning of the word were tied directly to the letters, then their meanings would be the same. It's the linguistic convention that stands above the letters that determines the meaning of those letters. And a linguistic convention needs a mind as its source, not matter.[16] Again, the mind of God is the best explanation for why linguistic conventions exist.

There's also the evidence from the presence of design, which points to the need for an Intelligent Designer. If you were to find a watch lying on the ground, because of the obvious presence of the design in the mechanism of that watch, you would not think it had come about by chance or by some gradual evolutionary process but instead that it had been designed by a designer. Biologist Michael Denton wrote that if we were to magnify a cell a thousand times, "What we would then see would be an object of

15. Collins, *Language of God*, 1–2.
16. Pearcey, "Phillip Johnson Was Right."

unparalleled complexity and adaptive design."[17] Since it makes sense to surmise that a designer designed a watch, it also makes sense to surmise that an ultimate Designer designed the complexity of biological cells.

Then, too, there is evidence that an unseen, immaterial, objective, moral reality exists and that the most likely place where such an immaterial, moral reality can exist is in the mind of a holy God who can not only make distinctions between right and wrong but is the ultimate standard of what is morally right. How can we know that such a moral reality exists? By understanding what a truth-maker is. Consider the following two statements:

1. This rose is red.
2. It is wrong to rape young girls.

What makes the first statement a true statement? It's when the rose is in fact red. The truth-maker of the first statement is the observable, empirical fact that the rose is red. The statement is true because it corresponds to an external, objective reality. This is called the correspondence theory of truth, which says that "a belief or statement is true only if it matches with, reflects, or corresponds to the reality it refers to."[18] The statement itself is a truth-bearer because it states a fact that is true. What is a "truth-maker"? It's a fact that makes a statement true. The facts that support the truth of a sentence are its truth-makers.

I assume you would agree that the second sentence—It is wrong to rape young girls—is making a statement that is true. What, though, makes that statement true? What is the truth-maker of that statement? It's not the observable act itself that makes the second statement true. Why not? Because the rightness or the wrongness of an act is not something that can be observed. Philosopher Douglas Groothuis wrote, "We don't verify the wrongfulness of murder in the same way we verify an individual fact of history; nonetheless, meaningful statements about morality are true or false, depending on whether they match the moral law."[19]

So, again, what makes the second statement true? What is its "truth-maker"? What makes it true is that it is pointing to an objective, moral truth.

---

17. Denton, *Evolution*, 328.
18. Lewis, *Mere Christianity*, 123.
19. Groothuis, *Christian Apologetics*, 124.

If the "truth-maker" of that statement does not reside in an observable reality, then in what kind of reality does it reside? In an unseen and immaterial moral reality. This idea is called "moral realism."

Where would such an unseen moral reality most likely reside? It needs to reside somewhere, does it not? Even though it's immaterial, it can't reside in a nothingness. Where is the most likely place that immaterial truths about morality reside? In the mind of a holy God.

The following are some other truths that follow from the truth-maker of that statement. First, there is a transcendent nature to the moral truth in that statement—it is wrong to rape young girls—that stands above all cultures and perspectives.

Second, the moral truth of that statement has an objective nature to it. It stands as true even if there were never an actual occurrence of rape. Even more, if someone were to say that it is in fact right to rape young girls, we would not consider their perspective to be an equally valid assertion; we would judge them as being morally wrong.

Third, it is knowable. The second statement is speaking of a reality that is knowable. Even though people question moral absolutes, they know in their hearts there is such a reality and that there is such a thing as right and wrong. This becomes manifestly clear when a moral relativist is treated unfairly. Try stealing from someone who has just stolen from you. Try lying to someone who has just lied to you. Their reaction will inevitably reveal their inherent belief in moral absolutes. C. S. Lewis wrote, "Whenever you find a man who says he does not believe in a real Right and Wrong, you will find the same man going back on this a moment later. He may break his promise to you, but if you try breaking one to him he will be complaining 'It's not fair' before you can say Jack Robinson."[20] As the Bible says, "[People] show that the requirements of the law are written on their hearts" (Romans 2:15).

Fourth, the truth of the statement reveals that the individual being raped has inherent rights that are being violated. The person who has been violated has standing as a person and therefore has value as a person.

To summarize, what we see in the second statement is a moral reality that

1. is unseen;
2. is immaterial;

---

20. Lewis, *Mere Christianity*, 6.

3. serves as a sufficient foundation for the moral ought; not merely what *is* the case, but what *ought* to be the case;

4. is able to distinguish between good and evil, right and wrong;

5. is transcendent to all cultures and perspectives;

6. is objective;

7. is knowable;

8. provides a foundation for the value of the individual.

The existence of such a moral reality is further evidence that a transcendent, absolutely real, holy, immaterial God who is mind and spirit and who has personal attributes exists.

Perhaps no single point of evidence or argument is enough to convince you of the existence of God. Consider, though, their cumulative force. This was enough to convince a thoroughgoing skeptic and unbeliever named Larry Sanger, a cofounder of Wikipedia. He described himself in this way: "Throughout my adult life, I have been a devotee of rationality, methodological skepticism, and a somewhat hard-nosed and no-nonsense (but always open-minded) rigor. I have a Ph.D. in philosophy, my training being in analytic philosophy, a field dominated by atheists and agnostics. Once, I slummed about the fringes of the Ayn Rand community, which is also heavily atheist."[21] In the following quote, though, Sanger talks about the strength of the arguments for God's existence when taken together:

> Individually, the arguments might seem relatively weak. As I said, the Argument from Contingency only shows that a necessary being exists. The Argument from Causality shows only that the universe had a cause outside of itself. The Argument from Design shows only that the universe has some sort of designer or other. ... But what happens when we combine all the arguments to make a unified case for the existence of God . . . ? Taken together, the arguments point to a necessary being that exists apart from space, time, and matter. This is the very cause of the universe, which was designed according to orderly abstract laws. Ever more complex properties emerge, one from another, with great beauty and rationality—rationality that exhibits various mind-like features. This order can be described as *good* . . . because life and its preservation seem to be part of the plan, and life is the very standard of value.[22]

21. Sanger, "Skeptical Philosopher."
22. Sanger, "Skeptical Philosopher"; emphasis in original.

When all the evidence and arguments are put together, then the case for God's existence is quite strong.

The Burden of Proof Doesn't Go in Only One Direction

The burden of proof for the existence of God should not fall only one way, though. Consider what atheists are implying by denying God's existence. By contending that there is no evidence for a Creator God, atheists are saying

1. that something comes from nothing;
2. that life comes from non-life;
3. that our minds and the vast amount of information in our DNA come from mindless matter;
4. that order and design come from random chaos;
5. that morals flow from a non-moral universe where there is no ultimate standard of goodness;
6. that we as persons have value even though there is no metaphysical foundation for that value;
7. that our meaning comes from a meaningless world.

In other words, atheists believe that an effect can be greater than its cause. Where, though, is their proof for such beliefs? As defenders of the Christian faith, Norman Geisler and Frank Turek have stated the position of the atheists well in the title of their book *I Don't Have Enough Faith to Be an Atheist*. The question as to where the universe came from is sufficiently answered only by a self-existent God who has the personal attributes needed to create a universe that has obviously been designed and has the kind of infinite power to create a universe out of nothing. Such a God is exactly the metaphysical foundation we need for our existence.

For Further Reading

The following are some suggested readings if you would like to pursue the subject of the evidence and arguments for the existence of the Creator further:

PART II: *DISCOVERING ONE'S TRUE SELF*

- Stephen Meyer, *Return of the God Hypothesis: Three Scientific Discoveries That Reveal the Mind Behind the Universe*. Dr. Meyer holds a PhD from the University of Cambridge in the philosophy of science and directs the Center for Science and Culture at the Discovery Institute in Seattle, which is devoted to making the case for intelligent design. Especially relevant is the chapter titled "The God Hypothesis and the Beginning of the Universe." Dr. Meyer has also written a book titled *Signature in the Cell: DNA and the Evidence for Intelligent Design*, which points to the need for a Designer to explain the presence of design and information in our DNA.

- Robert Spitzer, *New Proofs for the Existence of God: Contributions of Contemporary Physics and Philosophy*. A challenging but satisfying read that argues for the existence of God from the necessity of an unconditioned reality (a reality that does not depend on anything outside itself for its existence) and the presence of design in the universe.

- Lee Strobel, *The Case for a Creator: A Journalist Investigates Scientific Evidence That Points Toward God*. Lee Strobel set out to disprove Christianity after his wife became a believer, but in the process he became convinced that Christianity is true. In this book Strobel interviews several experts in relevant scientific fields (cosmology, physics, astronomy, biochemistry, biological information) all of whom say that the evidence points to the need for a Creator. Mr. Strobel is a prolific writer who has written a number of books that argue for the truth of Christianity, including *The Case for Christ*, *The Case for Christmas*, *The Case for Easter*, and *The Case for Faith*. His most recent book is *Is God Real? Exploring the Ultimate Question of Life*.

- Douglas Groothuis, *Christian Apologetics: A Comprehensive Case for Biblical Faith* (second edition). Dr. Groothuis presents a strong accumulative case for the existence of God (fine tuning, beauty, intelligent design, morals, consciousness), including a chapter on the universe having a beginning and therefore needing a cause (chapter 11: "Cosmological Arguments: A Cause for the Cosmos"). *Christian Apologetics* has become one of the most valuable resources there is for those Christian believers who want to learn how to defend their faith.

- Kenneth Boa and Robert Bowman Jr., *20 Compelling Evidences That God Exists: Discover Why Believing in God Makes So Much Sense*. The most relevant chapters include "The Evidence of Existence: The Most Elementary Question: Why Is There Something Rather than Nothing?" (chapter 3) and "The Evidence of the Universe's Beginning: The Universe Hasn't Always Been Here, and It's a Good Thing, Too" (chapter 4).

- Norman Geisler and Frank Turek, *I Don't Have Enough Faith to Be an Atheist*. Geisler and Turek present a wide range of evidence for the truths of the Bible, including who Jesus claimed to be, his resurrection, and the authenticity of the biblical record. Chapter 3 ("In the Beginning There Was a Great SURGE") is the most relevant to the matter of the universe having been created from nothing. SURGE is an easy-to-remember acronym: *S* for the second law of thermodynamics, *U* for the universe is expanding, *R* for radiation from the big bang, *G* for great galaxy seeds, and *E* for Einstein's theory of general relativity.

- William Dembski, Casey Luskin, and Joseph Holden (general editors), *The Comprehensive Guide to Science and Faith*. As the title says, this book is comprehensive. It covers almost any question you might have about the relationship between science and faith. The chapters are manageable. The book is written by experts in their field. The most relevant chapter for our purpose of pointing to the need for a Creator is "How Should Christians Think About Origins" (chapter 44) by Richard Howe. The book also has extensive sections on the presence of design in nature, the body, and the universe, and the inadequacies of the theory of evolution.

- William Lane Craig, *On Guard: Defending Your Faith with Reason and Precision*. The strength of this book is its clarity and how it walks the reader through the arguments step-by-step. The relevant chapters for our purposes are "Why Does Anything At All Exist?" (chapter 3) and "Why Did the Universe Begin?" (chapter 4). Chapter 5 on fine tuning is excellent as well ("Why Is the Universe Fine-Tuned for Life?").

- Paul Copan and William Lane Craig, *Creation out of Nothing: A Biblical, Philosophical, and Scientific Exploration*. A comprehensive discussion concerning the doctrine of *creatio ex nihilo* (creation from nothing).

PART II: *DISCOVERING ONE'S TRUE SELF*

Questions for Personal Reflection or Group Discussion

1. What is an infinite regression, and why is it an impossibility?
2. Why does the question "Who created God?" not make sense?
3. Besides self-existence, what are the other attributes of God that follow from him being the Creator?
4. How convinced are you that God exists by the evidence and arguments given in this chapter? Are there evidence and arguments that are more convincing to you? If so, what are they?

The Blessings of Fearing God

8

Seeing God: God Will Dwell with Us

AFTER HAVING TAKEN A brief interlude to look at the evidence and arguments for God's existence, I want us to pick up again on the subject of this book—being fulfilled by fearing God.

Now Show Me Your Glory!

In chapter 3 (Defining One's True Self: A Freedom or a Burden?) we looked briefly at Moses saying to God, "Now show me your glory" (Exodus 33:18). I want to take a deeper dive into Moses' request. The context is that of Israel having formed an idol in the shape of a golden calf and then worshiping it. They did this abominable act even though they had experienced the miraculous way in which God had delivered them from their slavery in Egypt (the ten plagues). They also did it even though God had miraculously delivered them from the Egyptian army who had pursued them to the Red Sea where the Israelites had no avenue of escape. The Red Sea was on one side, and the Egyptian army was on the other. What did God do? He parted the waters of the Red Sea so the Israelites could walk across on dry land. When the Egyptian army pursued them, God closed the waters, and the entire army was drowned. Even though the Israelites had seen the mighty hand of God, they still worshiped an idol that they had to have known was not the God who had delivered them. God was so incensed by their idolatry that he told Moses he would not go with the Israelites on their journey to the promised land "because you are a stiff-necked people and I might destroy

SEEING GOD: GOD WILL DWELL WITH US

you on the way" (Exodus 33:3). Moses, however, was able to convince God to go with them because he reminded him that they were God's people and that God's presence was what set them apart from all the other nations. So God relented and said he would go with them, not because he was pleased with the people but because he was pleased with Moses: "I will do the very thing you have asked, because I am pleased with you and I know you by name" (Exodus 33:17).

It was at that point that Moses said, "Now show me your glory" (Exodus 33:18). When everyone else was worshiping idols, Moses bucked the trend of his fellow Israelites and even of his own brother, Aaron, by pursuing his relationship with God. Why? What was he looking for? And what did he mean by "glory"? What is God's glory?

Moses' request to see God's glory comes out of the blue. One commentator said that Moses was asking for further confirmation from God that he would indeed go with them. It seems, though, that Moses' request goes deeper than that in that Moses is asking for a next-level—really, an ultimate-level—knowledge of God. Matthew Barrett writes, "Moses seems to be asking for something that goes well beyond anything he's ever experienced before."[1]

The key to understanding what Moses was asking for is understanding what God's glory is. It has to do with his luminosity or light, but that light has to do with much more than the kind of light that comes from the sun. The glory or light of God has to do with who he is, with his attributes, his character. For example, the apostle John wrote, "God is light; in him there is no darkness at all" (1 John 1:5). John is speaking metaphorically, not literally, and is describing God's moral character. He's saying that God is absolutely good, holy, truthful, and righteous. There is absolutely no moral darkness in him. There is a parallel passage in the Gospel of John: "This is the verdict: Light has come into the world, but people loved darkness instead of light because their deeds were evil. Everyone who does evil hates the light, and will not come into the light for fear that their deeds will be exposed. But whoever lives by the truth comes into the light, so that it may be seen plainly that what they have done has been done in the sight of God" (John 3:19–21). That passage makes it clear that "light" is referring to moral light. So when we're talking about the glory of God, one aspect of it is the absolute moral purity of God.

---

1. Barrett, *None Greater*, 18.

In another passage God's light is spoken of as being life: "In him [Jesus] was life, and that life was the light of all mankind" (John 1:4). Later, John talks about Jesus being "the light of life" (John 8:12). Life has to do not only with God bringing us into existence but also with our being in relationship with God for eternity. As Jesus said, "Now this is eternal life: that they may know you, the only true God" (John 17:3), where "know" is a term that speaks of our intimate and eternal relationship with God.

The point is that God's glory has to do not only with the light of God but also with the fullness, completeness, and perfection of his attributes, character, and power. When Moses said, "Now show me your glory," he was asking to see God in all his infinite fullness. It was a bold request. It took a lot of courage to make that request. So why did Moses do it? Because he realized that seeing God was where he would find ultimate fulfillment and satisfaction.

What We Need to Understand About Seeing God

We need to understand something, though, and that is that seeing God is very different from merely looking at something in everyday experience. If we think that seeing God is no different than merely looking at a sunset, watching a movie, or observing a science experiment, we're wrong. Seeing God is entirely different. It's in a category all by itself. It's different in at least four ways.

First, it's different because seeing God means knowing God on a deep level relationally. To see God is to engage with him relationally on every level of our being—emotionally, intellectually, and volitionally. It's knowing God with both the mind and the heart. Theologian David Vandrunen writes about when Moses said, "Now show me your glory," saying that "this 'man of God' (cf. Deut 3:1) *rightly desired even greater communion with his Lord.*"[2] By asking to see God's glory, Moses was asking for a deeper relationship with him.

Second, seeing God is different from merely looking at something because seeing God transforms us. It changes us on a deep level. It changes us from the inside out. After Moses' experience of seeing God in the cleft of the rock (we'll talk about this in a bit), he spent forty days and forty nights in the presence of the Lord on Mount Sinai. During that time, Moses felt no need to eat food or drink water; God himself was the source of

---

2. Vandrunen, *God's Glory Alone*, ch. 3; emphasis added.

his sustenance. When Moses descended from Mount Sinai, "his face was radiant because he had spoken with the LORD" (Exodus 34:29). Being in God's presence transformed Moses physically, causing his face to glow. The Israelites were afraid to even approach him. As a result, Moses put a veil over his face. Paul, referring back to that veil in a contrasting way, writes that "we all, who with unveiled faces contemplate the Lord's glory, are being transformed into his image with ever-increasing glory, which comes from the Lord, who is the Spirit" (2 Corinthians 3:18). That glory is coming from inside us because of the transforming power of the Holy Spirit giving us new life.

Third, seeing God is extremely dangerous. As finite creatures, we simply can't withstand seeing the infinite God. As Moses learned, it can cause death. When God told Moses, "You cannot see my face, for no one may see me and live" (Exodus 33:20), he was speaking literally, not metaphorically. There is a reason the apostle Paul wrote that God "lives in unapproachable light" (1 Timothy 6:16). It's because the infinite being of God is indeed unapproachable by us who are finite creatures.

Fourth, seeing God is different from merely looking at something in everyday experience because it compels worship. That's why when the seraphim—the angels made of fire—look at God, they worship him by singing, "Holy, holy, holy" (Isaiah 6:3). That's also why all throughout the book of Revelation, seeing God and worshiping him go hand in hand; one does not appear without the other. For example, it says of "the four living creatures" who surround the throne of God, "Day and night they never stop saying: 'Holy, holy, holy is the Lord God Almighty, who was, and is, and is to come'" (Revelation 4:8). Then, too, the apostle John saw those in heaven who had been victorious over persecution worshiping and singing, "Who will not fear you, Lord, and bring glory to your name? For you alone are holy" (Revelation 15:4). Their motivation for worshiping God was not because they were commanded to but because they were compelled to. The compulsion to worship rose inexorably from within them when they saw God. Seeing God drew worship out of them. It was a natural response. The same should be true of us because, just like fearing God, worshiping God is what we were made to do. It should be our natural response.

PART II: *DISCOVERING ONE'S TRUE SELF*

Fearing God and Seeing God Are Related

Why am I talking about seeing God in a book that is primarily about fearing God? Because fearing God and seeing God are integrally related to each other. They're related in that both contain at their core the three attitudes as to what it looks like to fear God: utter dependence, undivided attention, and unshakable trust.

We see the connection between fearing and seeing God in the way that God answered Moses' request to see his glory: "Now show me your glory" (Exodus 33:18). God gave Moses the following instructions for how he could see God: "There is a place near me where you may stand on a rock. When my glory passes by, I will put you in a cleft in the rock and cover you with my hand until I have passed by. Then I will remove my hand and you will see my back; but my face must not be seen" (Exodus 33:21-23). In this experience of seeing God, Moses experienced all three aspects of what it looks like to fear God. First, he experienced *utter dependence* in that the God who revealed himself to Moses was the Creator of all things, the I Am,[3] the self-existent One on whom Moses was utterly dependent for his existence. God had to protect Moses from his infinite glory by shielding Moses with his hand and showing only his back. Second, he experienced *undivided attention* in that the vision of God grabbed Moses' attention, and nothing could possibly distract him from even this partial view of God. Third, he experienced *unshakable trust* in that Moses was trusting that the God who said, "No one can see me and live" would not destroy him. Moses was defenseless against this God. He was trusting completely in the grace of this dangerous God. Even though the word "fear" does not appear in this passage, it was still a fear-of-God experience. It was also a seeing-God experience, thereby connecting both the fear of God and seeing God.

I need to point out that what I'm contending here is that even though a biblical passage does not contain the words "fear of God," if it contains the aspects of what it looks like to fear God—utter dependence, undivided attention, and unshakable trust—it is then a passage that can help us understand the many facets of fearing God.

There are two differences between fearing God and seeing God, though. First, fearing God is of this age, whereas seeing God takes place

---

3. When God revealed himself to Moses in the burning bush, he said that his name was "I Am" (Exodus 3:14), which means the self-existent One, the One who has existence within himself.

primarily in the age to come. Second, we fear God with the eyes of faith now, but we will see God with the eyes of "glorified sight" later.[4]

The Beatific Vision

There is a teaching in Christian theology called the beatific vision. The word "beatific" is related to the word "beatitude" and comes from a Latin word that means "blessed." The beatific vision, therefore, refers to "the blessed vision," which is the hope that we will be able to gaze directly at the infinite beauty of the God who is the source of all beauty and blessing. Samuel Parkison, in his book *To Gaze upon God*, defines the beatific vision in this way: "The beatific vision ... is the sight of God himself. The beatific vision is God's incomprehensible and ineffable glory beheld directly."[5]

Is it not true that seeing God is our greatest and ultimate desire and hope? After all, what could possibly be greater, more ultimate, and more fulfilling than seeing God, who is the one who made us in his image so we could be in a relationship of love with him for eternity? Nothing! God has "set eternity in the human heart" (Ecclesiastes 3:11), and because of that, we have a deep-seated desire for eternity. Only the infinite, eternal God can fulfill that desire, and only he can fulfill us for all eternity on every level of our being—emotionally, intellectually, relationally, spiritually, and physically. Parkison wrote, "That blessed vision is the culmination of all our godly enjoyments in this life and the satiation of all our desire."[6] I like that phrase "the satiation of all our desire." To be satiated means to be fully and completely satisfied, and only an infinite and eternal God can fully and completely satisfy us for all eternity. King David, the author of most of the psalms in the Bible, wrote, "One thing I ask from the LORD, / this only do I seek: / that I may dwell in the house of the LORD / all the days of my life, / to gaze on the beauty of the LORD / and to seek him in his temple" (Psalm 27:4). The beatific vision is that gaze that David craved. It was the one thing that David asked for, the one thing that he sought. What mattered most to David was to see the face of the beautiful, awesome God.

---

4. Terminology taken from Parkison, *To Gaze upon God*, ch. 4.
5. Parkison, *To Gaze upon God*, ch. 1.
6. Parkison, *To Gaze upon God*, ch. 1.

PART II: *DISCOVERING ONE'S TRUE SELF*

A Dilemma

For those of you who have been reading closely, you might have picked up on a dilemma, or a point of tension between two things. How can seeing God offer the promise of ultimate fulfillment and blessedness while at the same time be extremely dangerous such that it inevitably causes death? How can we reconcile those two conflicting ideas? How can we reconcile the fact that seeing God is dangerous ("No one may see me and live") with the fact that we are compelled to worship God when we see him because we are drawn to him as the one who will fulfill our ultimate purpose both in this present life and in the one to come?

To answer the question of how to reconcile the dangerous nature of seeing God with the fulfilling nature of seeing him, I invite you to look with me at how the apostle John describes the holy city of God that will come down from heaven at the end of human history and the beginning of eternity. It's a city where, at last, God himself will dwell in the very midst of his people: "I did not see a temple in the city, because the Lord God Almighty and the Lamb are its temple. The city does not need the sun or the moon to shine on it, for the glory of God gives it light, and the Lamb is its lamp" (Revelation 21:22–23). Remember that we're looking at this passage to answer the question as to how seeing God can hold the promise of ultimate fulfillment and blessedness while at the same time being extremely dangerous such that it inevitably causes death. Paul, moreover, adds in the following two verses another level of difficulty when it comes to seeing God, which is the invisibility of God: "Now to the King eternal, immortal, *invisible* . . ." (1 Timothy 1:17, emphasis added), and "God, the blessed and only Ruler, the King of kings and Lord of lords, who alone is immortal and who lives in unapproachable light, whom no one has seen *or can see*" (1 Timothy 6:15–16, emphasis added). God is invisible to us.

Jesus as the Lamp

The answer to our questions about resolving the tension between the danger of seeing God and the blessing of seeing God, and about how we can see the invisible God, comes down to Jesus Christ. Notice especially these words in that same passage in Revelation: "For the glory of God gives it light, and the Lamb is its lamp." The Lamb, who is Jesus Christ, is the visible lamp through which we will see the glory of God, which, as we talked about before, is the fullness and perfection of the character and attributes of God. Consider, too, where John says, "No one has ever seen God, but the one and only Son [referring to Jesus], who is himself God and is in closest relationship with the Father, has made him known" (John 1:18). Jesus is able to reveal God to us because he is both fully God and fully man.

When Jesus came to earth, the incomprehensible happened. The Infinite entered the realm of the finite. The Unlimited identified with those who are limited. The Artist of all paintings became one of his paintings. The Designer became one of the things that was designed. The Creator of all things joined the realm of his creation by taking on human flesh. Jesus became the Infinite-finite, the Unlimited-limited, the Artist-painting, the Designer-designed, the God-man.

Jesus as the Lamb

The problem of our not being able to see God is not only a matter of God being invisible and dangerous, but it's also a matter of our having broken our relationship with God. Remember that we talked about how seeing God is different from our merely looking at something. One of the ways it's different is that to see God means to engage with him relationally on every level of our being—emotionally, intellectually, and volitionally. It's knowing God with both the mind and the heart. As sinners, though, we have alienated ourselves from God. The Bible says, "Once you were alienated from God and were enemies in your minds" (Colossians 1:21). How is it that we have alienated ourselves from God?

Philosopher James K. A. Smith wrote, "We become what we worship because we worship what we love."[7] G. K. Beale wrote, "What we revere we resemble."[8] What those statements are implying is that we are by nature reflecting beings. We're "mirrors with wills," which was the topic of chapter 2 (We Are Mirrors with Wills), and the primary purpose of a mirror is to reflect. What do we reflect? We reflect that which is most important to us. As "mirrors with wills" we choose either to reflect ourselves or to reflect God. When we reflect ourselves, we become nothing but ourselves. When a work of art rejects the purpose for which it was made, which is to reflect the creativity of the artist, then it loses its purpose for existence. It then has no foundation for its value and no purpose as a work of art because it has lost

---

7. Smith, *You Are What You Love*, 23.
8. Beale, *We Become What We Worship*, 297.

its connection to and relationship with the artist. It has dismissed the artist as being unimportant and has thereby lost its own foundation for value and meaning. In and of itself, it is nothing. Its only purpose is to reflect the thoughts and emotions of the artist.

By choosing to reflect ourselves rather than God, we sever ourselves from the God who is the foundation for our identity, our meaning, and our value. When we reflect God, though, then we reflect the image of God in which we were made. We reflect a foundation that is able to uphold all of who we are. When we believe we have the power to define ourselves, on the other hand, we fail to live up to the purpose for which we were made, which is to reflect the glory of the Artist who made us. By reflecting ourselves, we place ourselves above our Creator, which causes our relationship with God to be broken, and that leads to both spiritual and physical death. As Paul wrote, "The wages of sin is death" (Romans 6:23).

What is the solution to our having broken our relationship with God? The solution is to have our relationship with God restored. How, though, can that happen? Being holy, God is just, and his justice demands that we pay the penalty of sin, which is death.

The solution to our sin problem is found in the image of Jesus as being the lamb. John the Baptizer described Jesus as "the Lamb of God, who takes away the sin of the world!" (John 1:29). And earlier in the book of Revelation, the apostle John described Jesus as "a Lamb, looking as if it had been slain, standing in the center of the throne" (Revelation 5:6). There are several practices in the Jewish religion that "the Lamb of God" refers to.

First, on the Day of Atonement, two goats were to be selected. One was to be sacrificed as a "sin offering" (Leviticus 16:9). Concerning the other goat, the priest was to then "lay both hands on the head of the live goat and confess over it all the wickedness and rebellion of the Israelites— all their sins—and put them on the goat's head" (Leviticus 16:21). This goat is called the "scapegoat." Having become identified with our sin, the scapegoat was to be led into the wilderness where it would die carrying the sins of the people.

Second, the lamb of God imagery referred to the Passover. The Passover had to do with the tenth, and last, plague that God visited on Egypt and the Israelites as God challenged Pharaoh to let his people go. God told Moses, "About midnight I will go throughout Egypt. Every firstborn son in Egypt will die" (Exodus 11:4–5). To prevent that from happening in their household, the Jews were to slay a lamb without defect and then

SEEING GOD: GOD WILL DWELL WITH US

"take some of the blood and put it on the sides and tops of the doorframes of the houses where they eat the lambs" (Exodus 12:7). When the Lord sees the blood on the door of the houses, the passage says, "I will pass over you" (Exodus 12:13).

The final image that the "Lamb of God" term referred to is the one that we covered in chapter 6 (Unshakable Trust: Trusting in the Goodness of the God Who Cares) where we talked about God commanding Abraham to sacrifice his son. Just as Abraham was about to plunge the knife into Isaac's chest, the Lord withheld his hand and provided a ram to be slain in Isaac's place: "Abraham looked up and there in a thicket he saw a ram caught by its horns. He went over and took the ram and sacrificed it as a burnt offering instead of his son. So Abraham called that place The LORD Will Provide" (Genesis 22:13–14).

To those of us with modern sensibilities of animal rights and of anthropomorphizing animals, the idea of killing an animal on our behalf seems barbaric. What kind of sick God would demand so much killing and blood to be appeased? Are we not beyond such gruesome barbarity? Haven't we matured as a culture beyond the need for bloody sacrifices in order to approach God? How can any civilized person still believe such voodoo-like hocus-pocus?

What if, though, the barbaric nature of those sacrifices is precisely the point? What if God is trying to shock us? What if he's trying to get our attention about the severity of our sin? The truth is, he is! Out of his grace, he's attempting to warn us against what sin does. The death of an animal for our sin is a sign as to what we deserve as a result of having broken our relationship with God.

Are we repulsed by the sacrifice of an animal? Good! We should be even more repulsed, though, by the breaking of our relationship with God because of our sin than we are of the killing of an animal on our behalf.

Thankfully, the penalty of death that we deserved to pay has been paid on our behalf, and it's been paid by God's one and only Son. Paul wrote, "The death he [Jesus] died, he died to sin once for all" (Romans 6:10). The author of the book of Hebrews wrote, "Unlike the other high priests, he [Jesus] does not need to offer sacrifices day after day, first for his own sins, and then for the sins of the people. He sacrificed for their sins once for all when he offered himself" (Hebrews 7:27). The gruesome nature of animal sacrifices has been done away with through Jesus, the "Lamb of God, who takes away the sin of the world!" (John 1:29).

PART II: *DISCOVERING ONE'S TRUE SELF*

As we looked at the images of the lamb in the Old Testament, we saw three recurring themes. First, *justice*: death is the price that must be paid because of our having broken our relationship with God. Second, *identification*: our sin is placed on the lamb, and as a result, the lamb becomes identified with our sin. Third, *substitution*: the lamb, having become identified with our sin, pays the price for sin on our behalf.

Jesus, through his dying on our behalf for our sins, covered all three of those themes:

- "He [the Messiah] was pierced for our transgressions, he was crushed for our iniquities; the punishment that brought us peace was on him, and by his wounds we are healed. We all, like sheep, have gone astray, each of us has turned to our own way; and the LORD has laid on him the iniquity of us all" (Isaiah 53:5–6).
- "The Son of Man [Jesus] did not come to be served, but to serve, and to give his life as a ransom for many" (Matthew 20:28).
- "God made him [Jesus] who had no sin to be sin for us, so that in him we might become the righteousness of God" (2 Corinthians 5:21).
- "But God demonstrates his own love for us in this: While we were still sinners, Christ died for us" (Romans 5:8).
- "God presented Christ as a sacrifice of atonement, through the shedding of his blood—to be received by faith. . . . He did [this] to demonstrate his righteousness at the present time, so as to be just and the one who justifies those who have faith in Jesus" (Romans 3:25–26).

How can Jesus' substitutionary sacrifice be applied to us? God himself applies to us what Christ did on our behalf as we, through faith, are identified with Jesus Christ. Another term for being identified with Christ is to be "with Christ" or "in Christ." Notice the terms "with Christ" and "in Christ" in the following passage. Notice, too, how our being placed "in Christ" happens as we place our faith and trust in Christ:

> But because of his great love for us, God, who is rich in mercy, made us alive *with Christ* even when we were dead in transgressions—it is by grace you have been saved. And God raised us up *with Christ* and seated us *with him* in the heavenly realms *in Christ Jesus*, in order that in the coming ages he might show the incomparable riches of his grace, expressed in his kindness to us *in Christ Jesus*. For *it is by grace you have been saved, through faith*—and this

not from yourselves, it is the gift of God—not by works, so that no one can boast." (Ephesians 2:4–9, emphasis added)

Our being reconciled to God comes entirely through the payment of death that Jesus paid on our behalf and is received by faith alone. Our being made right with God is not based at all on our own merit.

Paul spells out even more the amazing implications of our identification with Christ in the following passage:

> Or don't you know that all of us who were baptized into Christ Jesus were baptized into his death? We were therefore buried with him through baptism into death in order that, just as Christ was raised from the dead through the glory of the Father, we too may live a new life.
>
> For if we have been united with him in a death like his, we will certainly also be united with him in a resurrection like his. For we know that our old self was crucified with him so that the body ruled by sin might be done away with, that we should no longer be slaves to sin—because anyone who has died has been set free from sin.
>
> Now if we died with Christ, we believe that we will also live with him. (Romans 6:3–8)

Baptism, which is to be immersed into something, is a vivid picture of what it means to be identified with Christ. We usually associate baptism with being immersed into water, but the baptism of this passage in Romans is a waterless baptism. It's instead being immersed into, or identified with, the death of Jesus Christ. That is to signify our dying to our sin nature. It's to release us from the power of and enslavement to sin. But the picture of baptism doesn't end there. Through our baptism into, or identification with, Christ, we are joined with Jesus Christ not only in his death but also in his resurrection from the dead. We are joined with him to a new life that is entirely free from the prospect of death. This is resurrection life, which is eternal life. As Jesus said, "I have come that they may have life, and have it to the full" (John 10:10).

How is this identification possible? It's possible through the Holy Spirit who indwells the person who trusts in Christ. We see this truth pictured in the image of a severed branch being grafted into a life-giving tree. What that image signifies is that as we become identified with Christ by placing our faith and trust in him, the Holy Spirit gives us new life just like a tree gives life to a branch that has been grafted into it. The Holy

Spirit transforms us from death to life. The Holy Spirit, who was involved with the creation of the universe (Genesis 1:2), now gives us new life as we become identified with Christ. As Paul wrote, "If anyone is in Christ, the new creation has come: The old has gone, the new is here!" (2 Corinthians 5:17). Previous translations of the NIV (such as the 1984 version) word this as "If anyone is in Christ, *he is a new creation*" (emphasis added). I prefer this understanding when reading the passage, as it makes it clear that it is we ourselves, as individuals, who are the new creation.

Transformed to Have Open Access to God

As we place our faith and trust in Jesus Christ, not only is our relationship with God restored, our rebellion against God forgiven, our fear of death removed, and we are infused with the life-giving power of the Holy Spirit, but we are also given the power to be transformed into the image of the one who made us in his image. Paul wrote we "are being transformed into [Jesus'] image with ever-increasing glory, which comes from the Lord, who is the Spirit" (2 Corinthians 3:17–18). This is an inside-out transformation. When we place our faith in Jesus, the process of being transformed into his image begins immediately through the transforming power of the Holy Spirit who gives us the power to become like Christ.

The Answer to the Dilemma

Jesus is the answer to the dilemma as to how seeing God is both dangerous and fulfilling. As we are identified with Christ, our sins are paid for. Justice has been done. What Jesus did on our behalf on the cross took care of our being prevented from seeing God because of our having been alienated from him because of our sin. Through Jesus, our relationship with God has been restored.

When our relationship with God is restored through our faith in Christ, our journey toward eternal fulfillment has only begun. Now we have something to hope for, a future to hope for. That future is being in a relationship of love with God for eternity. As Paul wrote, "May the God of hope fill you with all joy and peace as you trust in him, so that you may overflow with hope by the power of the Holy Spirit" (Romans 15:13). God is the God of hope, and that hope should give us joy and peace. Indeed, the Holy Spirit will cause that hope to overflow within us.

SEEING GOD: GOD WILL DWELL WITH US

What exactly, though, do we hope for? We hope for the final, ultimate, and eternal answer to our dilemma that is found in the holy city of God that, at the end of history, will come from heaven down to earth so that God himself will dwell among those who have been transformed so they could be in God's presence. This will take place after all idolators and demons had been banished to eternal separation from God. It will also take place after the new heavens and the new earth have replaced the old heavens and earth. The apostle John wrote about this holy city in the final two chapters of the Bible:

> I did not see a temple in the city, because the Lord God Almighty and the Lamb are its temple. The city does not need the sun or the moon to shine on it, for the glory of God gives it light, and the Lamb is its lamp. . . .
>
> Then the angel showed me the river of the water of life, as clear as crystal, flowing from the throne of God and of the Lamb down the middle of the great street of the city. On each side of the river stood the tree of life, bearing twelve crops of fruit, yielding its fruit every month. And the leaves of the tree are for the healing of the nations. No longer will there be any curse. The throne of God and of the Lamb will be in the city, and his servants will serve him. They will see his face, and his name will be on their foreheads. There will be no more night. They will not need the light of a lamp or the light of the sun, for the Lord God will give them light. And they will reign for ever and ever. (Revelation 21:22–23, 22:1–5)

There is so much that could be said about this passage, but the one aspect that I want to focus on is the presence of God. The presence of God is seen in every aspect of this vision.

A temple is where the presence of God is. The holy city, though, does not need a temple because the entire city serves as the temple because of the presence of "the Lord God Almighty and the Lamb."

The "river of the water of life" is mentioned. Biblical commentator G. K. Beale writes that "the water metaphor primarily *represents the life of eternal fellowship with God and Christ.*"[9]

The holy city does not need the sun or moon because God himself and the Lamb will be its light. Beale writes that the main point of that language "is that nothing from the old world will be able to hinder God's glorious

---

9. Beale and Campbell, *Revelation*, "The New Creation and the Church Perfected in Glory"; emphasis added.

presence from completely *filling the new cosmos or the saints from unceasing access to that divine presence.*"[10]

Whereas God had told Moses, "You cannot see my face, for no one may see me and live" (Exodus 33:20), in the holy city we "will see his face." This is to fulfill the blessing that was to be given by the priests to Israel but now applied to all those, including gentiles, who trust in the Lord: "The Lord bless you and keep you; the Lord make his face shine on you and be gracious to you; the Lord turn his face toward you and give you peace" (Numbers 6:24–26). Even though in the holy city we will see God's face, the finite-infinite divide will always be there. That means, though, that we will know God for all eternity and never tire of knowing him.

The fact that "his name will be on their foreheads" refers to when the priest entered the holy of holies once a year. They would engrave the words "Holy to the Lord" on a gold plate and fasten it to a turban worn by the priest, which meant that it was on the priest's forehead (Exodus 28:36–38). Having God's name on the believer's forehead signifies that we each are now priests who are qualified to enter into God's presence not by our own merit but by what Christ has done on our behalf. It also signifies safety and belonging.

In the holy city there's life, life, and more life, and absolutely no death. The curse of death, which includes the threat of being separated from God, will be entirely removed. John wrote, "He will wipe every tear from their eyes. There will be no more death or mourning or crying or pain, for the old order of things has passed away" (Revelation 21:4). To emphasize how the holy city is filled with life, John wrote, "On each side of the river stood the tree of life, bearing twelve crops of fruit, yielding its fruit every month" (Revelation 22:2). If the tree of life bears fruit, how much more will we who are made in God's image and are in a full relationship with him bear fruit?

Finally, to complete this journey through how we will have full access to God in the holy city and to highlight the intimacy that will be true of our relationship with God, I must make you aware of what the holy city is called. John wrote, "I saw the Holy City, the new Jerusalem, coming down out of heaven from God, prepared as *a bride* beautifully dressed for her husband" (Revelation 21:2, emphasis added); "One of the seven angels who had the seven bowls full of the seven last plagues came and said to me, 'Come, I will show you *the bride, the wife of the Lamb*'" (Revelation

---

10. Beale and Campbell, *Revelation*, "The New Creation and the Church Perfected in Glory"; emphasis added.

21:9, emphasis added). The holy city is called "the bride, the wife of the Lamb." That image raises thoughts of how intimate the relationship is between God and those in the holy city.

The Fear of God Fulfilled

The holy city is the culmination and fulfillment of fearing God. As King Solomon wrote, "Now all has been heard; here is the conclusion of the matter: Fear God and keep his commandments, for this is the duty of all mankind" (Ecclesiastes 12:13). In the holy city, our fearing God will not be done in the context of struggle, strife, and doubt. Instead, we will be so overwhelmed with the majesty and splendor but also the love and provision of God, that we will be overcome with the urge to worship him, which is what fearing God is all about.

I have defined fearing God as acknowledging that God alone is God and as being overwhelmed by his splendor. We have also looked at how fearing God consists of the three aspects of utter dependence, undivided attention, and unshakable trust. All of that is here in the holy city.

In the holy city, there will be no question that God alone is God and that he consists of three persons. Let me remind us that a "person" is a being, whether infinite or finite, uncreated or created, who possesses personal attributes such as emotions, an intellect, and a will and is able to participate in interpersonal relationships with other persons. It's significant that, in the following verse, there is only one throne and that each of the three persons of the Trinity—God the Father, Jesus the Lamb, and the Holy Spirit as the water of life—are part of it: "The river of the water of life, as clear as crystal, [flows] from the throne of God and of the Lamb down the middle of the great street of the city" (Revelation 22:1–2). We will be so overwhelmed by seeing God in all his glory and by being in a constant relationship with him that the thought of worshiping any other god will never enter our minds.

Concerning what it looks like to fear God, all three aspects are there. Our *utter dependence*, depicted by thirst, will be there. The Holy Spirit says this by way of invitation: "Let the one who is thirsty come; and let the one who wishes take the free gift of the water of life" (Revelation 22:17). This is like what Jesus told the Samaritan woman at the well: "Whoever drinks the water I give them will never thirst. Indeed, the water I give them will become in them a spring of water welling up to eternal life" (John 4:14). In the holy city we will be aware of our utter dependence on God as a form of thirst, and, as we drink the life-giving water of the Holy Spirit, our souls will experience both extreme joy and unforgettable relief.

There will also be *undivided attention*, both the kind that fear demands and the kind that love calls for. Fear demands our undivided attention in that we can't possibly look away from the object of fear. That's what being in the presence of the majestic God who surrounds us with his light will be like. But there will also be the undivided attention that love calls for because the Lamb who sits on the throne has loved us with an everlasting love, and that love will fulfill our every longing.

Then, too, *unshakable trust* will be there. We will be filled with the overpowering realization of the absolute goodness and trustworthiness of God. We will experience his undeniable love at a depth we had never known before. We will know without a shadow of a doubt that God is one who provides all things for us on every level of our being. And we will know that we belong, that we are a part of his family, and that, as Paul wrote, "neither death nor life, neither angels nor demons, neither the present nor the future, nor any powers, neither height nor depth, nor anything else in all creation, will be able to separate us from the love of God that is in Christ Jesus our Lord" (Romans 8:38–39).

What We Will Be

The apostle John wrote, "Dear friends, now we are children of God, and *what we will be has not yet been made known*. But we know that when Christ appears, we shall be like him, for we shall see him as he is" (1 John 3:2, emphasis added). When we place our faith in Jesus, the process of being transformed into God's image begins immediately through the transforming power of the Holy Spirit. That transformation gives us the ability to see Jesus "as he is." But seeing Jesus "as he is" will also transform us into what "has not yet been made known." Thomas Andrew Bennet writes, "Bearing witness to great beauty or great ugliness has transformative impact. . . . [The apostle] John imagines that this [transformative] principle will apply in toto when we are confronted by the unvarnished beauty of Christ at his arrival. Seeing him 'as he really is' indicates that up until that time, human eyes will not really have apprehended the full beauty and divinity of eternal life and that when we do, the sight will overwhelm and change them."[11] We need to be transformed to see Jesus, and then when we do see Jesus, we

---

11. Quoted in Parkison, *To Gaze upon God*, ch. 2.

will be further transformed—"the sight will overwhelm and change them." Beauty transforms; infinite beauty transforms eternally. John wrote that "what we will be has not yet been made known." I contend that what we will be has to do with our experiencing eternal and overwhelming joy and peace in each of the three aspects of what it looks like to fear God. We will be completely fulfilled in our *utter dependence* on God, in our giving him our *undivided attention*, and in having an *unshakable trust* in him. Why do I say that? Because, as we have seen in the Gospels and as we will see in Philippians 2, that's what Jesus was like.

Questions for Personal Reflection or Group Discussion

1. Why is seeing God dangerous? Why is it fulfilling?
2. What does it mean for Jesus to be depicted as a lamp?
3. What does it mean for Jesus to be depicted as a lamb?
4. What is our sin problem? How is it related to our being "mirrors with wills"?
5. How is the dilemma of seeing God as being both dangerous and fulfilling reconciled in Jesus?
6. How can we become identified with Christ?
7. What are your thoughts and reactions to what the holy city will be like?

9

Fearing God: Bringing Healing to Our Fractured Culture

W<small>E</small> <small>LIVE</small> <small>IN</small> <small>AN</small> extremely divided, polarized, and fractured culture. There seems to be no common ground between the factions in our culture. Everyone is pointing their fingers at someone else and blaming them for the troubles our culture is experiencing. Pundits in both political parties accuse the other side of being divisive. There seems to be no room for reconciliation and no interest in restoring broken relationships.

In his book *Love Your Enemies*, Arthur Brooks, former president of the American Enterprise Institute and a professor both at the Harvard Kennedy School and at the Harvard Business School, writes, "Political differences are ripping our country apart. . . . Political scientists find that our nation is more polarized than it has been at any time since the Civil War."[1] The root cause for our polarization, according to Brooks, is one word: contempt. The different factions have contempt for each other. What is contempt? Brooks answers that question in the following way: "Social scientists define contempt as anger mixed with disgust. These two emotions form a toxic combination, like ammonia mixed with bleach. In the words of nineteenth-century philosopher Arthur Schopenhauer, contempt is 'the unsullied conviction of the worthlessness of another.'"[2] Those are strong words and strong feelings. But is Brooks wrong in how the different factions in our culture feel toward each other? I don't think so.

---

1. Brooks, *Love Your Enemies*, 2.
2. Brooks, *Love Your Enemies*, 10.

Fearing God: Bringing Healing to Our Fractured Culture

Can fearing God bring healing to our broken and polarized culture? To answer that question, I want us to look at how the apostle Paul recommended that a church suffering from divisions could find healing.

Divisions Within the Church

The apostle Paul founded the church in the city of Philippi in AD 51. Regrettably, divisions formed in the church within ten years of its founding.[3] One of the reasons Paul wrote his epistle, or letter, called Philippians to the church was to address those divisions and to encourage the believers to maintain their unity. What he had to say to the Philippians is helpful in learning how to approach the divisions in our own culture.

Paul uses two phrases to refer to why there were divisions in the church. The first phrase is "selfish ambition," which refers to the factions that were developing in the church, and the second phrase is "vain conceit," which refers to the prideful attitude of certain individuals that caused them to have a higher regard for themselves than was warranted. One commentator writes that some people in the church "were creating factions based on personal prestige, drawing away members and creating parties. Their *conceit*, that is, their excessively favorable opinion of themselves or their abilities, caused them to place themselves above others."[4] Biblical commentator J. B. Lightfoot writes that the problem in the church had to do with "the exaltation of party and the exaltation of self."[5] That sounds like a fairly accurate description of what is causing division, discord, and disharmony in our own culture—factions and egos.

What is Paul's advice? "Do nothing out of selfish ambition or vain conceit. Rather, in humility value others above yourselves" (Philippians 2:3). Walking in humility is the answer to the things that cause us to be divided. What is humility? It's to "value others above yourselves." Paul clarifies what he means by that statement in the next verse: "Not looking to your own interests but each of you to the interests of others" (Philippians 2:4). To "value others above ourselves" means that we are to live for others, that we are to put their interests before our own. In a very real sense, to live for others means we are to "fear" others, not in the sense of being afraid of them but in the sense of taking our focus off ourselves and turning it

---

3. Barton et al., *Philippians, Colossians, and Philemon*, 7.
4. Barton et al., *Philippians, Colossians, and Philemon*, 53.
5. Lightfoot, *St. Paul's Epistle*, 109.

toward others instead. That's what fearing God means—taking our focus off ourselves and focusing instead on God.

When Jesus washed the feet of the disciples, he gave a demonstration of servant leadership that shocked the disciples. Peter even protested, "No, you shall never wash my feet" (John 13:8). Washing someone's feet was something only a servant would do. Jesus then said, "'Do you understand what I have done for you?' he asked them. 'You call me "Teacher" and "Lord," and rightly so, for that is what I am. Now that I, your Lord and Teacher, have washed your feet, you also should wash one another's feet'" (John 13:12–14). As Jesus acknowledged, he was their Lord. He was not a Lord, though, who lorded it over others. Instead, he was a Lord who served others. His whole life was devoted to living for the interests of others.

Paul then illustrates what he meant when he said, "Each of you should look not only to your own interests, but also to the interests of others." He elaborated by saying, "In your relationships with one another, have the same mindset as Christ Jesus" (Philippians 2:5). Jesus gave us the ultimate example of living for the interests of others by living and dying sacrificially for us. Here's the passage: "[Jesus Christ,] being in very nature God, did not consider equality with God something to be used to his own advantage; rather, he made himself nothing by taking the very nature of a servant, being made in human likeness. And being found in appearance as a man, he humbled himself by becoming obedient to death—even death on a cross!" (Philippians 2:6–8).

What was Jesus' motivation for such a sacrificial act? It was his fear of God. This should not come as a surprise since the prophet Isaiah had written that the Messiah would "delight in the fear of the LORD" (Isaiah 11:3). Still, though, why do I say that Jesus was motivated by the fear of God since those words do not appear in this passage? I say it because all three aspects of what it looks like to fear God are found in this passage.

Utter Dependence: The passage says that Jesus "made himself nothing." The actual phrase is that of Jesus "emptying himself."[6] He emptied himself to the point of becoming a servant or a slave. The Greek term *doulou* can be translated either as "servant" or "slave". The stronger sense of "slave" is more correct here because the utter dependence involved in being a slave is what Paul was intending to communicate. Biblical commentator Frank Thielman

---

6. As Frank Thielman writes, "The phrase 'made himself nothing' is an appropriate translation of the Greek that says, more literally, 'he emptied himself' (NASB, NRSV)." *Philippians*, 117.

writes, "The slave in Greco-Roman society was deprived of the most basic human rights. In the same way, Christ refused to exploit the privilege of his deity and giving up that right became a slave."[7] A slave was utterly dependent on his master. In the same way, Jesus was utterly dependent on his Father. Jesus' utter dependence was not oppressive as one would think a slavish dependence would be, though. Instead, it was Jesus' joy; it meant life to him. To mention a previous analogy again, being utterly dependent on the breathing apparatus when scuba diving is not oppressive; it's life.

When it comes to talking about Jesus being utterly dependent on his Father, I'm reminded of our discussion about the verse in the psalm: "Let all the earth fear the LORD; / let all the people of the world revere him. / For he spoke, and it came to be" (Psalm 33:8–9). That verse says that we should fear God because he created us out of nothing. Our being created from nothing speaks of how we are utterly dependent on our Creator for our very existence. When the passage in Philippians says that Jesus "made himself nothing" and became a slave, it was not saying that he was made from nothing, as we are, but that he voluntarily chose to not exercise his divine prerogatives and to live in utter dependence on his Father.

Undivided Attention: The passage in Philippians says that Jesus "humbled himself." What does it mean to be humbled? It means to live in constant awareness of who we are as persons living in the context of the God who is to be feared. God told the Israelites, "If my people, who are called by my name, will humble themselves and pray and seek my face and turn from their wicked ways, then will I hear from heaven, and I will forgive their sin and will heal their land" (2 Chronicles 7:14). That verse is a good explanation of what it means to be humble because it describes humility with the words of praying and seeking his face. Those words—praying and seeking—speak of how we are to give God our undivided attention. In another passage, the prophet Micah talks about how we are "to walk humbly with [our] God" (Micah 6:8). To walk with someone is to be in their presence and to be aware of them at all times. This is what Jesus did. Jesus said of himself, "Very truly I tell you, the Son can do nothing by himself; he can do only what he *sees his Father doing*, because whatever the Father does the Son also does" (John 5:19, emphasis added). Jesus' attention was constantly on the Father. Why? Because Jesus' passion was to glorify the Father by doing his will.

---

7. Thielman, *Philippians*, 117–18.

Unshakable Trust: The passage in Philippians says that Jesus became "obedient to death—even death on a cross!" (Philippians 2:8).

How far are you willing to go when obeying someone? The answer to that question indicates how much you trust them and believe that they are accurately representing the cause that you share with them. Many a soldier has followed his commander into seemingly certain death because they believed in the worthiness of the cause and trusted their leader.

Jesus knew exactly what God's purpose for his life was. Referring to himself as the "Son of Man," he said, "The Son of Man did not come to be served, but to serve, and to give his life as a ransom for many" (Matthew 20:28). Jesus was willing to obey his Father even to the point of giving his life for us.

So we see that Jesus exhibited all three aspects of what it looks like to fear God and that motivated him to love us to the extent of dying on our behalf for our sins.

Let me remind us that Paul was pointing to the example of Jesus' life as the paradigm for how to address divisions within the church. Paul wrote the following just prior to talking about what Jesus did: "Do nothing out of selfish ambition or vain conceit. Rather, in humility value others above yourselves, not looking to your own interests but each of you to the interests of others. In your relationships with one another, have the same mindset as Christ Jesus" (Philippians 2:3–5). Jesus' relentless focus on God by fearing his Father caused him to live for others and even to give his life for them. It caused him to seek the best for others, to put the interests of others first. Can you imagine if we each lived our lives in that way, lived with Jesus' mindset or attitude toward others? Our world would be so different if we lived not with selfish ambition but with the ambition of lifting up, encouraging, and looking out for the interests of others. How, though, can we get there? We live in such a divided and fractious culture. I'm suggesting that the fear of God is relevant to our situation. We're going to look at each aspect of what it looks like to fear God—utter dependence, undivided attention, and unshakable trust—and discuss how the fear of God can bring healing to our culture.

Utter Dependence Both Humbles and Unifies Us

One of the aspects of fearing God is to realize that we are utterly dependent on God for our existence. God did not create us as extensions of the impersonal force of his being, but instead spoke us into existence from nothing by his powerful word of creation. John wrote of Jesus, "In the beginning was the Word. . . . Through him all things were made; without him nothing was made that has been made" (John 1:1, 3). The realization that we were made from nothing should shock us into humility. Being utterly dependent on God for our existence means there is no place for pride, no place for puffing ourselves up, and no place for boasting before God. It should cause us to fear God, which means to acknowledge that God alone is God and that he alone is worthy of our worship.

Besides causing us to be humbled before God, the realization that we are utterly dependent on God for our existence should also give us a deeper foundation for our feeling unified with others than does the idea that we share a common humanity, as important as that is. Arthur Brooks cites the work of Robert Putnam in his book *Bowling Alone: The Collapse and Revival of American Community*. In that book, Putnam talks about what he calls "bridging social capital," which is "built on our common humanity; it emphasizes how we are alike rather than how we are different."[8] He then applied that sense of "common humanity" to the problems of "breaking" and "othering." What "breaking" and "othering" have in common is that they create "a hard line between 'us' and 'them' by making any kind of difference—whether skin color, socioeconomic status, political views, or anything else—a dividing line. The danger of othering, says john,[9] is that we end up making caricatures of others because we never come into contact with them—and once we go down that road, he cautions, 'we're not a long way from doing all kinds of terrible things to each other.'"[10]

Brooks writes that there is an alternative to "breaking" and "othering," and that is Putnam's "bridging": "Rather than pushing away the 'other' because of differences, bridging initiates contact. While it does not demand that we set aside every point of difference, bridging at its core *does* demand that we see and acknowledge the other person's humanity. It does not ignore difference, but it gives pride of place to what we hold in common."[11] Brooks is saying that the way to address the stark differences

---

8. Brooks, *Love Your Enemies*, 118.

9. The name "john" refers to john a. powell, who is the professor of law and African American studies and ethnic studies at the University of California, Berkeley. He prefers to not capitalize the first letters in his name.

10. Brooks, *Love Your Enemies*, 120.

11. Brooks, *Love Your Enemies*, 121; emphasis in original.

between us is by focusing on our "common humanity" and on "what we hold in common." I agree that such an approach is valuable, but I'm also saying that we need to go deeper than that to heal the divisions between us. We need to find something that gets our attention, that moves us, and that even has the power to transform us. The idea that we are each utterly dependent on God for our existence can do that.

By way of an analogy, imagine two lights—a lamplight and a night-light—in a five-year-old girl's bedroom, and they're arguing about who's the most important. The lamplight boasts, "I'm the most important because I illuminate the entire room so that she can see to run and play without running into things and getting hurt. Also, her parents can read to her by my light so she can learn about the world and all that's in it." The night-light responds by saying, "I'm the most important because my softer light allows her to sleep at night so she can have the energy to play. Also, I provide just enough illumination so she can find her parents at night when she's scared." Then the mother steps into the room and flips the switch that turns off both lights. That's when the two lights realize that they would be nothing apart from the electrical power that energizes them. They are each utterly dependent on that power. That realization shocks them into a sense of humility and causes them to stop looking at themselves; they instead look at their utter dependence on their source of power. They stop boasting and find unity by being humbled in the face of realizing that they are nothing apart from the source of power that empowers them. They find meaning and fulfillment not in themselves but in glorifying their source of power who made them for their particular purpose—one to be a lamplight and the other to be a night-light.

The same should be true of us. Realizing that we are utterly dependent on God for our existence should shock us into walking humbly with God, and that in turn should give us a deeper and more motivating reason for feeling unified with others. The creating and sustaining power of God's word is our power source. Apart from the creating and sustaining word of God, we are nothing. That should humble us and cause us to feel unified with others.

Undivided Attention Should Cause Us to Live for Others

The undivided attention that is part of what it looks like to fear God means taking our focus off ourselves and placing it squarely on God, and that should in turn cause us to focus on others rather than on ourselves. Through the undivided attention aspect of fearing God, we will gain a passion for others.

When Jesus was asked what the greatest commandment is, he replied, "'Love the Lord your God with all your heart and with all your soul and with all your mind.' This is the first and greatest commandment. And the second is like it: 'Love your neighbor as yourself'" (Matthew 22:37–39). It's no coincidence that loving one's neighbor follows loving God. Jesus' priority of commandments follows the Ten Commandments, where the first four (do not have other gods before God; do not make an idol; do not misuse God's name; devote yourself to God on the Sabbath) are focused on our relationship with God, and the last six are focused on how we are to live rightly with others (honor your father and mother; do not murder; do not commit adultery; do not steal; do not give false testimony; do not covet). Jesus' life is an example of how we are to live for others as we place our undivided attention on God. Consider, for example, one of theologian Miroslav Volf's basic theological commitments, or truths, as expressed by Matthew Croasmun and Ryan McAnnally-Linz in *Envisioning the Good Life*: "Jesus says in John: 'As I have loved you, you should also love one another' [13:34 NRSV], *not* the reciprocal 'As I have loved you, you should love me.'"[12] Reciprocal love is how we normally function: If I love you, then it is expected that you will love me. Jesus is saying, instead, that because he loves you, then go and love others as he has loved you. As the apostle John wrote, "We love because he [God] first loved us" (1 John 4:19).

A True Story of Living for Others

We are inspired by stories of people turning their attention away from themselves and living sacrificially for the sake of others, especially when those stories are true. Nelson Mandela is one such true story. Mandela committed himself to living sacrificially for the cause of winning freedom for his fellow Black people from the oppressive government of South Africa. He committed his life for the cause of freedom, and paid the price.

The Union of South Africa was formed in 1910. While *apartheid*, which means "apartness," had been the unofficial policy of the ruling white class in South Africa for centuries, it became official in 1948 when the National Party, which had its roots in the Dutch settlers, gained

---

12. Volf, *Exclusion and Embrace*, epilogue; emphasis and brackets in original.

control of the government from the United Party, which had its roots in the English settlers.

In 1950 the National Party passed the Group Areas Act. Mandela labeled this act "residential apartheid" because it meant that "each racial group could own land, occupy premises, and trade only in its own separate areas."[13] It also meant that whites could declare a particular community or piece of land to be white property and forcibly take it. The National Party separated the races not only by territory but also in other respects. The Reservation of Separate Amenities Act of 1953 declared that Black people must use separate bathrooms, schools, and hospitals.[14]

It was into this kind of racist culture that Nelson Mandela, the future president of South Africa, was born and lived, causing him to devote his life to the cause of freedom for his people. To accomplish that end, he joined the African National Congress (ANC). The ANC was "a huge coalition of different political philosophies, views, and attitudes. Founded in 1912, it grouped a range of African leaders who combined to resist their exclusion from political power," including their right to vote.[15] While the ANC was initially committed to using nonviolent means of protest (e.g., strikes, stay-at-homes, boycotts) to denounce the racist policies, such tactics were proving ineffective, and the increasingly oppressive and militaristic push-back by the white National Party eventually caused them to resort to using sabotage, which is the strategy where they destroyed structures but resolved not to hurt people. They called the new branch of the ANC that used this strategy the "Umkhonto we Sizwe," which means the "spear of the nation," and called it the MK.[16] Nelson Mandela was asked to head up the MK. This new assignment meant that he had to separate himself from his family and friends to go into hiding by going underground, taking on an assumed name and a new identity, and moving about in a clandestine manner.

For almost a year and a half, he read literature on guerrilla warfare, traveled throughout other countries to promote the cause of freedom in South Africa, and received military training in those countries.[17] Soon after returning to South Africa, the police found him, arrested him, put him on trial, convicted him, and sentenced him to five years in prison. After

---

13. Mandela, *Long Walk*, ch. 14.
14. Revell, *Apartheid*, "Apartheid and Its Consequences."
15. Tutu, *No Future*, ch. 3.
16. Mandela, *Long Walk*, ch. 42.
17. The following draws from Mandela, *Long Walk*, ch. 47–49.

having served nine months of that sentence, the police discovered the MK headquarters at Rivonia, arrested the other members of the MK team, and put them in the same prison where Mandela was serving his sentence. Their trial, which included Mandela, started in October 1963, and most of them were found guilty on June 11, 1964. Sentencing would take place the next day. Toward the beginning of the trial the counsel for the State had told Mandela and the others that they would be seeking the death penalty.

On Friday, June 12, tensions both in and around the courthouse were high. Security was out in full force. The courtroom was packed. Two thousand people stood outside the courthouse holding banners saying things like "We stand by our leaders." Mandela was fully expecting to be sentenced to death. Judge de Wet showed them leniency, however, and sentenced them to life in prison.

During Mandela's time in prison, the struggle for freedom for the Black people in South Africa continued. Nations around the world pressured South Africa to end the policy of apartheid by placing economic sanctions on the country.

When F. W. de Klerk took over as South Africa's president following the resignation of pro-apartheid P. W. Botha, he began to dismantle the policies of apartheid and subsequently removed the ban on the ANC, thereby making it a legal organization.[18] He also approved the release of Mandela from prison on February 11, 1990. All told, Mandela spent twenty-seven years in prison. Four years later, on April 27, 1994, a hugely momentous occasion took place. For the first time in South African history, Black people were allowed to vote in a national election. Even though Mandela had been a citizen of South Africa since birth, it was the first national vote that he had ever cast. The African National Congress received 62 percent of the vote, which meant that Mandela would assume the office of the president. His primary goal as president was not only to unite the country but also to heal it.

While my intension is not to idealize Nelson Mandela (he had his faults, as do we all), I want to recognize how his life is an inspirational example of what it looks like to give one's life for the sake of others. He lived with an overwhelming passion for the freedom of others. To a large extent, he lived for others, not for himself. Sadly, he sacrificed his first marriage and the joy of watching his family grow up so he could devote himself to the struggle for liberation in South Africa. Mandela embodied

---

18. For the changes in leadership, see Mandela, *Long Walk*, ch. 98.

Paul's admonishment to "look not only to your own interests, but also to the interests of others" (Philippians 2:4).

As much as Mandela is an example of living for others, Jesus is even more. Indeed, he's our ultimate example of living for others. He left his throne in heaven to join those on earth who are enslaved to sin and death. He left eternity to live in time. As the Creator of all things, he became part of creation by taking on human flesh. Most importantly, as the Source of life he took on death so that we could have life. He did all that because he placed his attention entirely on God, and that undivided attention on God caused him to live for others. It's hard to imagine how much our world would change if we were to have an undivided attention on God and to then be motivated to live sacrificially for the good of others like Jesus did.

Unshakable Trust Is the Soil We Need to Nourish Our Souls

Unshakable trust in God is another of the aspects of fearing God. Our unshakable trust in God is based on the fact that he is absolutely good and infinitely powerful, and is therefore worthy of our trust.

We concluded the chapter about unshakable trust (chapter 6, Unshakable Trust: Trusting in the Goodness of the God Who Cares) by looking at these verses: "The LORD Almighty is the one you are to regard as holy, he is the one you are to fear . . . , and he will be a holy place [or sanctuary]" (Isaiah 8:13–14a). A sanctuary is a place where we can find rest, peace, and safety for our souls. We can find rest for our souls because God is the greatest power that exists—and is therefore to be feared—and because he is good, trustworthy, and caring. God is worthy of our unshakable trust, and that unshakable trust will give rest for our souls.

The Condition of Our Souls

We don't often stop to think about the condition of our souls, and yet the condition of our souls is vitally important to how well we live our lives.

What is the condition of your soul? Is it troubled? Is it filled with anxiety? Is it angry, resentful? Or is it at a place of rest and peace and filled with joy? The psalmist wrote, "Blessed are those who fear the LORD. . . . They will have no fear of bad news; their hearts are steadfast, trusting in the LORD" (Psalm 112:1, 7). Do you have a "steadfast" heart, or is it easily shaken? When we have an unshakable trust in the Lord, our souls will be protected from "the fear of bad news," no matter what the form of that bad news takes. Having an unshakable trust in the goodness and power of God is the key to having a steadfast heart and to protecting our souls.

Jesus was protective of his soul and advised us to be so as well. Consider, for example, how Jesus could tell us, "Love your enemies and pray for those who persecute you" (Matthew 5:44). We have a hard time understanding the reasoning behind Jesus' teaching. Here's how we're tempted to respond to Jesus' words: "How can I possibly love my enemies? They have wronged me! They don't deserve my love! What they deserve is my anger, my blame! If I love them, then they win, and I lose. They will feel free to walk all over me!"

If Jesus' words are put in the context of a concern for the spiritual health of the soul, though, then they make perfect sense. Then we understand that Jesus is saying, "Don't be enslaved by a hatred for your enemies. If you hate them or resent them, then they own you. Because of your hatred, you become enslaved to your enemies. Be concerned for the state of your soul. Be aware of what your attitudes toward your enemies are doing to your soul. Praying for your enemy frees you from enslavement. Praying for them maintains your humanity. Praying for them heals your soul."

Nelson Mandela was someone who was concerned about the state of his soul. It would be completely understandable if he had harbored thoughts and feelings of hatred toward those who had been responsible for having kept him in prison for twenty-seven years. He sacrificed so much because of what the racist South African government did to him. And yet here is how he responded to President Bill Clinton's question about whether he hated those who had kept him in prison for so long: "Absolutely I did. . . . I was angry. And I was afraid, because I had not been free in so long. But [on the day of my being released from prison] as I got closer to the car that would take me away, I realized that when I went through that gate, if I still hated them, they would still have me. I wanted to be free. And so I let it go."[19] He was guarding his soul. The best way to guard the health of our soul is by planting it in the soil of unshakable trust in the goodness and power of the God who is to be feared.

---

19. Mandela, *Long Walk*, foreword.

PART II: *DISCOVERING ONE'S TRUE SELF*

Blame Damages the Soul

One of the most common threats to the soul is when we blame others for our suffering and troubles. Denis Liam Murphy writes in his book *The Blame Game*, "Blame isn't just about finding fault for something we think has gone wrong; it is holding someone responsible for the way we feel. Blame creates attachment to someone else being the reason we feel the way we do."[20] Murphy is saying that blame goes beyond merely "finding fault" to labeling someone in the entirety of their identity as being guilty. It rejects seeing them in their wholeness as persons made in the image of God and instead reduces their identity to that single act of how they have harmed us. That harmful or hateful act becomes, to us, their entire identity. As a result, we are filled with resentment, distrust, anger, and hatred toward them. When blame becomes the soil in which our souls are planted, our soul will die by the poison in that soil. We instead need to plant our souls in the soil of a God who is good, forgiving, loving, caring, and restorative, a God in whom we can have an unshakable trust.

Blame has an agenda, and that agenda is to declare ourselves the innocent victim and others the guilty perpetrator. Our victimhood mentality can deceive us by causing us to think that anything we do as victims to exact revenge is excusable. We allow our victimhood status to excuse doing to the perpetrator whatever they did to us, and perhaps even worse. By seeing ourselves as the innocent victim and the perpetrator as guilty, we are tempted to put ourselves in the place of judge, jury, and executioner.

We must protect our own humanity—our souls—at all costs, though. We must not allow the hate and dehumanization waged against us to cause us to become like those who have acted out of their inhumanity. Even when others have dehumanized us, we must not dehumanize them in return. That is hard, obviously, but we must look at forgiving others as being a matter of maintaining the health of our souls. We must refuse to allow the soil of hatred to poison our souls. The problem, though, is that we don't have the power within ourselves to do that because blame comes so naturally to us. Not only can we not think of any other way to live, we can't even imagine any other way. When we are struggling to forgive, we need to declare our utter dependence on God to change our hearts. As we take our attention off the object of our blame and place it on the love that God has shown us through Jesus Christ, God will change our hearts through the power of the

---

20. Murphy, *Blame Game*, ch. 1.

Holy Spirit. Declaring our utter dependence on God to change our hearts can be a constant, minute-by-minute battle.

Retribution Versus Restoration

I'm not denying that there is a place for blaming others. What I'm saying is that we need to be aware of how blame harms our souls. We can temper the damaging effects of blame by blaming others in a restorative way rather than a retributive way. What's the difference? There are several differences.

First, the agenda of retributive blame is to declare oneself as innocent and the other as guilty. It's to justify oneself at the expense of the other. Restorative blame, on the other hand, recognizes the guilt of the other, but it does so in such a way that prevents us from being enslaved to hatred, anger, and resentment.

Second, the goal of retributive blame is to punish the guilty. The goal of restorative blame is to reconcile the relationship and to restore the guilty back into the community, as difficult as that might be. The sense of community is the value that is the most important with restorative blame.

Third, the effect on the soul of retributive blame is to kill the soul by encouraging us to hold onto the hatred, anger, and resentment that enslaves us. The goal of restorative blame is to protect the soul by allowing forgiveness into our lives, which releases us from being enslaved to hatred, anger, and resentment.

I'm basing my ideas of retributive blame and restorative blame on Archbishop Desmond Tutu's concepts of retributive justice and restorative justice. After Nelson Mandela became South Africa's president in 1994, he established the Truth and Reconciliation Commission (TRC). Tutu, who headed up the TRC, used the idea of restorative justice to bring healing to South Africa following the destructive and divisive years of apartheid. The task of bringing healing to South Africa was challenging, to say the least. It seemed, at first, that there were only two alternatives. First, they could simply "let bygones be bygones"[21] and move forward from that point. Tutu wrote about the weakness of that approach: "Our common experience in fact is the opposite—that the past, far from disappearing or lying down and being quiet, has an embarrassing and persistent way of returning and haunting us unless it has in fact been dealt with

---

21. Tutu, *No Future*, ch. 2.

adequately. Unless we look the beast in the eye we find it has an uncanny habit of returning to hold us hostage."[22]

Second, they could seek out the perpetrators, take them to court, expose their guilt, and bring them to justice. The problem with this approach was not only that it would be costly and time-consuming, but also that it would not bring healing. It would cause the perpetrators either to go silent or to lie outrightly about their involvement, leaving the victims with no sense of closure and often no knowledge as to what had happened to their loved ones.

The TRC came up with a third alternative, which was to grant "amnesty to individuals in exchange for a full disclosure relating to the crime for which amnesty was being sought."[23] The goal of this third way was to heal, to reconcile, and to restore, and thus it came to be known as restorative justice. Restorative justice was based on the African concept of *ubuntu*. *Ubuntu* goes to the core of what it means to be human, and the most important part of what it means to be human is to belong to a community. *Ubuntu* includes concepts such as "My humanity is caught up, is inextricably bound up, in yours";[24] "A person is a person through other persons"; and "To dehumanize another inexorably means that one is dehumanized as well."[25] Tutu explains *ubuntu* in this way: "A person with *ubuntu* . . . has a proper self-assurance that comes from knowing that he or she belongs in a greater whole and is diminished when others are humiliated or diminished, when others are tortured or oppressed, or treated as if they were less than who they are. . . . To forgive is not just to be altruistic. It is the best form of self-interest. What dehumanizes you inexorably dehumanizes me. It gives people resilience, enabling them to survive and emerge still human despite all efforts to dehumanize them."[26] I want to highlight two sentences in the above quote: "To forgive is not just to be altruistic. It is the best form of self-interest." Those words speak of guarding our hearts and our souls.

Marietta Jaeger is a mother who modeled those words as she realized that she needed to care for her soul in the midst of a situation that could not have been more tragic. While she, her husband, and five children were camping in Montana, their seven-year-old daughter, Susie, was kidnapped

---

22. Tutu, *No Future*, ch. 2.
23. Tutu, *No Future*, ch. 2.
24. Tutu, *No Future*, ch. 2.
25. Tutu, *No Future*, ch. 3.
26. Tutu, *No Future*, ch. 2.

and murdered. The following are her words of how she worked through the struggle to forgive her daughter's murderer:

> I had finally come to believe that real justice is not punishment but restoration, not necessarily to how things used to be, but to how they really should be. In both the Hebrew and Christian scriptures whence my beliefs and values come, the God who rises up from them is a God of mercy and compassion, a God who seeks not to punish, destroy, or put us to death, but a God who works unceasingly to help and heal us, rehabilitate and reconcile us, restore us to the richness and fullness of life for which we have been created. This, now, was the justice I wanted for this man who had taken my little girl....
>
> Though I readily admit that initially I wanted to kill this man with my bare hands, by the time of resolution of his crimes, I was convinced that my best and healthiest option was to forgive. In the twenty years since losing my daughter, I have been working with victims and their families, and my experience has been consistently confirmed. Victim families have every right initially to the normal, valid, human response of rage, but those persons who retain a vindictive mind-set ultimately give the offender another victim. Embittered, tormented, enslaved by the past, their quality of life is diminished. However justified, our unforgiveness undoes us. Anger, hatred, resentment, bitterness, revenge—they are death-dealing spirits, and they will 'take our lives' on some level as surely as Susie's life was taken. I believe the only way we can be whole, healthy, happy persons is to learn to forgive. That is the inexorable lesson and experience of the gospel of Marietta. Though I would never have chosen it so, the first person to receive a gift of life from the death of my daughter ... was me.[27]

One of the many things that strikes me about Marietta's attitude is her concern for the spiritual health of her soul. She admitted that "initially I wanted to kill this man with my bare hands," but she eventually came to the conclusion that the "healthiest option was to forgive." Why? Because to retain "a vindictive mindset"—the mindset of blame—is a "death-dealing spirit" that robs one of life.

That kind of response to tragedy can't be done in a vacuum. It needs context. It needs a foundation. It needs a love and a forgiveness that so undergirds who we are that we are motivated to love and forgive others. That's what we find in the true story of how God loved us so much

27. Marietta Jaeger, as quoted in Tutu, *No Future*, ch. 7.

that he sent his Son to die on our behalf for our sins, and based on that substitutionary death, God forgives us and restores us into his family as a child who is deeply loved and who belongs, the ultimate *ubuntu*. When we place our unshakable trust in that kind of God, we will be planting our souls in the kind of soil that will nourish us so that we can live in a healthy way with whatever tragedy comes our way.

A Summary

In this chapter I claimed that fearing God can bring healing to our divided culture, and I looked at the relevance of each aspect of fearing God. First, being utterly dependent on God for our existence causes us to be humbled before God. It gives us a deeper foundation for our feeling unified with others than does the idea that we share a common humanity. Second, fearing God means taking our focus off ourselves and placing it squarely on God by giving him our undivided attention. As we love God, we should love others. Our outward focus toward God should cause us to focus on and to live for others rather than ourselves. This was the key application that the apostle Paul drew from Christ's life: You should "not [look] to your own interests but each of you to the interests of others. In your relationships with one another, have the same mindset as Christ Jesus" (Philippians 2:4–5). Third, the unshakable trust that we can find in the all-good and all-powerful God gives us the kind of nourishing and healing soil our souls need to flourish and to thrive in the midst of a toxic culture that is addicted to blaming each other. We need to guard our souls from being damaged and poisoned, and having an unshakable trust in the God who cares for and loves us with an overwhelming passion can help us do that.

If It Can Work in Football . . .

Football can be brutal not only physically but also when it comes to relationships. There's not only the competitive spirit between rival teams but also the fighting for positions within the team itself. That's why the College Football Playoff National Championship game between Ohio State and Notre Dame on Monday, January 20, 2025, stood out. Even ESPN's Scott Van Pelt and Rece Davis noticed the difference. Here's what they said: "We hear a lot of times people talk about their faith and people sort of dismiss it. [But the player's sharing their faith] became something powerful, not because they thought it was going to be handed to them to win a game, but it changed their relationships. It changed selfishness and made it go away. . . . We heard [Notre Dame coach] Marcus [Freeman] talk about that a lot this year . . . that it made guys selfless, and I think that's the power in it. It's not some magical thing . . . it helps you relate to your teammates differently."[28] That's exactly what Paul was saying should happen if we follow the example of Christ who feared God and selflessly gave his life for others. The players' fervency for their faith in Jesus Christ changed how they related to each other. It made their selfishness go away. That's what happens when we take our eyes off ourselves and place it on God, which is what fearing God is all about. It causes us to live selflessly, which is much needed in our fractured world.

Questions for Personal Reflection or Group Discussion

1. How does being utterly dependent on God for your existence affect you?
2. Are you less or more fulfilled when you live for others? Why?
3. Has your soul been damaged or poisoned? If so, how?
4. How will having an unshakable trust in God bring healing to your soul?

---

28. Stonestreet, "Everybody Was Talking"; ellipses and brackets in original.

Our Responses

10

Of What Should We Be Most Afraid?

WHEN YOU FIRST READ the words "fearing the infinite, loving, dangerous God" in the subtitle of this book, it's likely that the idea of being afraid of God was the first thought that came to mind. So let me ask the question, Is there a place for being afraid of God?

There is a place for being afraid of those things, including God, that can destroy us. Albert Martin writes in his book *The Forgotten Fear: Where Have All the God-Fearers Gone?*, "There is a legitimate sense in which the fear of God involves *being afraid of God, being gripped with terror and dread.*"[1] For one thing, there is the fear of we as sinners being exposed before the absolutely holy God. This is the kind of fear that Adam and Eve experienced in the garden after having disobeyed God. Adam said to God, "I heard you in the garden, and I was afraid because I was naked; so I hid" (Genesis 3:10). Then, too, there is being afraid of God in the sense of having a healthy respect for the infinite difference between his nature and ours. We as finite beings simply can't withstand the infinite nature of God.

I want to focus, though, on the words of Jesus when he said we should be afraid of God: "Do not be afraid of those who kill the body but cannot kill the soul. Rather, be afraid of the One who can destroy both soul and body in hell" (Matthew 10:28). Those are shocking words. They are serious words. They grab our attention. We need to understand what Jesus is saying. In particular, why did Jesus mention hell?

---

1. Martin, *Forgotten Fear*, ch. 2; emphasis in original.

The reason Jesus mentions hell is because hell is where we are eternally and relationally separated from God. Whereas physical death is where the soul is separated from the body, spiritual death is where we as persons are relationally separated from God for eternity.

The next question to ask, though, is, Who is doing the separating? God or us? Is God separating us from himself, or are we separating ourselves from him? Taken alone, the verse seems to be saying that God is the one banishing us to hell: "Be afraid of the One who can destroy both soul and body in hell." Yes, it's true that God can destroy us in hell, but is Jesus saying that God is the one sending us there? I don't think so. Why not? Because in another part of the New Testament, the apostle Peter said, "The Lord . . . is patient with you, *not wanting anyone to perish, but everyone to come to repentance*" (2 Peter 3:9, emphasis added). Then, too, a primary theme throughout the entire Bible is how God has given us the way by which we can have our relationship with him restored. The following three verses are only a few of the verses that speak of that truth:

- "But God demonstrates his own love for us in this: While we were still sinners, Christ died for us" (Romans 5:8).
- "This is love: not that we loved God, but that he loved us and sent his Son as an atoning sacrifice for our sins" (1 John 4:10).
- "God . . . reconciled us to himself through Christ" (2 Corinthians 5:18).

The term "reconciled" in that last verse means to restore a relationship where before there was enmity. Through the saving work of Jesus, God made it possible for our relationship with God to be restored. The implication of these verses then is that *we* are the ones who have separated ourselves from God, not the other way around. God is the one who has provided a way by which we can be restored in our relationship with him.

If God is not the one responsible for our being separated from him but has instead provided the way by which our relationship with him can be restored, then it must be that *we* are the ones responsible for separating ourselves from God. Is such alienation something we deserve, something we have brought on ourselves? Have we acted toward God in such a way that we deserve to be separated from him? As the apostle Paul wrote, we were the ones who were enemies of God: "Once you were alienated from God and were enemies in your minds because of your evil behavior" (Colossians 1:21–22).

Augustine, the fourth-century bishop, describes sin as *incurvatus in se*. What that Latin phrase means is that sin causes us to curve in on ourselves.[2] By curving in on ourselves, we replace God with ourselves and, consequently, break our relationship with God. The concept of *incurvatus in se* becomes especially clear when considered in the context of fearing God. One thing that fearing God does is to draw our attention away from ourselves and to focus it on the most important being there is, the one who alone is worthy of our worship, the one who created all things, the one who made us in his image so that we could be in a relationship with him. Sin is a failure to fear God, which is a failure to worship God alone. Sin causes us to worship ourselves, to reflect our own glory rather than God's glory. What we deserve because of such self-oriented thinking is the very separation from God that we yearn for. We want to be free from God so that we can be free to create who we imagine our true selves to be. We have turned our hearts toward the created order rather than to the Creator to find our meaning and identity. We assert that we have the power to define our own identity rather than to acknowledge our identity as persons made in the image of God. We believe that we can create our own purpose for life rather than having to live according to the purpose God has given us. We look for fulfillment by searching for the self we have defined for ourselves, which means creating ourselves in our own image rather than having a relationship with the transcendent God who created us in his image. We claim to be the ones who can create our own truth rather than to acknowledge God as the source of truth. We say that we can live by our own moral standards rather than acknowledging the moral standards given by God. If we do those things and have those attitudes, have we not separated ourselves from God? Have we not put ourselves in the place of God? Have we not raised the creation above the Creator? When we separate ourselves from God, he deals with us justly by granting us our wish. Alienation from him is precisely what we have asked for. Yes, God is the "One who can destroy both soul and body in hell" (Matthew 10:28), but we are the ones who have separated ourselves from God, and God grants us our desire to be separated from him.

God's Overwhelming Passion for Us

After having said that we should "be afraid of the One who can destroy both soul and body in hell," Jesus goes on to speak of why we should not

---

2. Villodas, *Good and Beautiful*, 3.

be afraid: "Are not two sparrows sold for a penny? Yet not one of them will fall to the ground outside your Father's care. And even the very hairs of your head are all numbered. So don't be afraid; you are worth more than many sparrows" (Matthew 10:29-31). What's going on here? How can Jesus say, on the one hand, that we should be afraid of the one who can destroy both body and soul in hell, but then, on the other hand, say we should not be afraid? What's going on here is that Jesus is talking about how God loves us, including both you and me, with an overwhelming passion. He's saying that we should be so overwhelmed with how much God loves and cares for us that the thought of being separated from him should be our greatest fear because it is the worst outcome that could possibly happen to us. Jesus follows up his statement about why we should be afraid of being separated from God in hell with two analogies, both of which are intended to overwhelm us with how much God cares for us and how God loves us with an overwhelming passion.

The first analogy is about two sparrows that have minimal monetary value. Jesus says that even though these two sparrows are insignificant monetarily, "not one of them will fall to the ground outside your Father's care." One biblical commentator wrote, "In some Greek usages, the word for 'fall' is translated as 'hop'—in which case a little sparrow cannot even hop on the ground without God's knowledge!"[3] It's amazing enough to think that God is aware of the deaths of two small sparrows, but to think that God is aware of even their hops is incomprehensible. It could very well be the case, though, that Jesus is indeed referring to the hops of sparrows because such detailed knowledge is in keeping with the next analogy.

In the second analogy Jesus talks about how God knows even the number of hairs on our head. Such knowledge astounds us. Even we don't know how many hairs we have on our head! In truth, we don't even care. And yet God knows us to such an extent that he knows those kinds of intimate details about us. That's how much God is aware of and cares for us. Read these beautiful words from King David: "For as high as the heavens are above the earth, / so great is his love for those who fear him; / as far as the east is from the west, / so far has he removed our transgressions from us. / As a father has compassion on his children, / so the LORD has compassion on those who fear him" (Psalm 103:11-13).

What is Jesus doing with these two analogies? He's saying that because God loves us with an overwhelming passion, we should be overwhelmed

---

3. MacArthur, *Matthew 8-15*, ch. 20.

with how much God cares for us. As a result, what we should be most afraid of is not God himself, but of being separated from him. Our being separated from him is not what he desires. His desire for each of us is to live in a relationship of love with him both now and for eternity. Being eternally alienated from the God who cares for us to an such unimaginable extent should be our greatest fear.

Questions for Personal Reflection or Group Discussion

1. When you read the words "fearing the infinite, loving, dangerous God" in this book's subtitle, what were your initial thoughts about what "fearing" meant?
2. What is your reaction to Jesus' two analogies—God being aware of the hopping of sparrows and of the number of hairs on our heads?
3. Are you afraid of being relationally separated from God? Why or why not?
4. What is your greatest fear?

11

The God to Be Feared Calls Us to Himself

THUS FAR, WE'VE SEEN some unexpected things as we have looked at what it means to fear God. We saw how Jesus talked about being "afraid of the One who can destroy both soul and body in hell" (Matthew 10:28), but then he made it clear that the greatest thing we should be afraid of is being separated from this God who cares for us down to the level of knowing the number of hairs on our heads. We saw how the God who says, "You cannot see my face, for no one may see me and live" (Exodus 33:20) is exactly the kind of God we need because only that kind of God will fulfill us for an eternity. We've seen how the way to find your true self is not by defining who you are but by letting go of how you define yourself and letting the God who made you in his image define you. We've seen how what at first appears to be the freedom of defining one's self is in fact a burden because there is no foundation on which to rest when it comes to knowing who you truly are. We've seen how teachers who begin by saying the most affirming things about us end up removing the foundation for our value and even our existence as persons.

We're about to look at another unexpected thing. You would think that a God who is to be feared is a God who wants to keep his distance from us and that we would want to keep our distance from him. In fact, though, the God who is to be feared calls out to us and draws us to himself. The God who is to be feared is a God who invites rather than repels. He does so through innumerable means; we will cover only a few of them.

God Calls to Us Through Our Longings

Jesus said, "I have come that they may have life, and have it to the full" (John 10:10b). Jesus becomes more explicit about what that full life means when he defines eternal life in this way: "Now this is eternal life: that they know you, the only true God, and Jesus Christ, whom you have sent" (John 17:3). Hidden within that verse are three words and phrases that speak of our longings. Because we're multileveled beings, we don't have only one longing; we have multiple longings. I will go through each of the words and phrases and talk about how they point to our longings and about how God fulfills each of those longings.

First is the word *eternal*. We long for eternity. Are our lives temporal or eternal? If this one life is all there is and we cease to exist after death, then where is our hope? Death brings futility and despair, and it causes us to ask the question, Does my life matter? Jesus said that our lives do matter. They matter not because we will live on through our legacy but that *we ourselves* will live on into eternity. There is hope for life beyond death; death does not have the final word. Jesus said, "I am the resurrection and the life. The one who believes in me will live, even though they die" (John 11:25). Those words carry meaning because Jesus conquered death by rising from the dead.

In his book *Forever: Why You Can't Live Without It*, Paul Tripp writes that part of what it means to be human is to long for eternity: "Longing for eternity doesn't mean you're spiritual; it simply means you are human. . . . This is not first a matter of what we believe; it is first a matter of who we are. Eternity lives and longs inside us; there is simply no escaping it. . . . This is why you and I struggle. Deep inside each of us is a cry for forever."[1] Why does this "cry for forever" exist in our hearts? Because God "has set eternity in the human heart" (Ecclesiastes 3:11).

Our longing for eternity was inadvertently confirmed by Dr. Corliss Lamont, a philosopher who was voted Humanist of the Year in 1977. What that honor meant was that he was a thoroughgoing atheist. As an atheist he vehemently denied that there is any immaterial part of us, such as a soul, spirit, or mind, that continues to exist after death. He considered such an idea to be "pathetic." And yet, in the process of writing about how he did not believe we continue to exist after death, he wrote, "Even I, disbeliever that I am, would frankly be more than glad to wake some day to a worthwhile

---

1. Tripp, *Forever*, ch. 1.

eternal life."[2] Now where did that thought come from? Certainly not from Lamont's atheistic belief system. As much as Lamont's atheistic, materialistic belief system caused him to deny it, there was still an unexplained part of him that yearned for more than what this life has to offer.

God calls to us through our longing for eternity, and the eternal God offers eternal life to us through our trusting in Jesus.

Second is the word *life*. The single word *life* fulfills two longings: our longing to be made whole and our longing to be transformed. What does it mean to be made whole? It means to be restored to our original, uncorrupted self, and to have that restoration take place on every level of our being—physically, spiritually, and emotionally. When Jesus healed people, he made them whole physically by giving sight to the blind, the ability to walk to the lame, and even life to the dead. He didn't just make people whole physically, though, he also made them whole spiritually. When four men carried their paralyzed friend to Jesus to be healed, the first thing Jesus said to the man was, "Friend, your sins are forgiven" (Luke 5:20). While Jesus did indeed heal the man physically later, his first act was to forgive his sins, thereby making the man whole spiritually.

Jesus also makes us whole emotionally by letting us know that God loves us[3] and that we belong to the family of God, thereby fulfilling our need for belonging.[4]

God calls to us through our longing to be made whole, and the God who has created us in his image is the only one able to make us whole!

Third is the word *life*. We long to be transformed. This is the second longing implied by the word *life*. The context of Jesus talking about life here is that of eternity—"eternal life." By saying that life is eternal, Jesus is not talking merely about a life that continues forever but without any moral change. While it's true that we find great satisfaction in many of our relationships now, we also experience jealousy, hurt, hatred, anger, rejection, being slighted, alienation, oppression, injustice, humiliation, depression, and despair. If our lives were to continue unchanged forever with no moral transformation, then they would be more like hell than heaven. For heaven to be heaven, we need to be morally transformed.

---

2. Lamont, *Philosophy of Humanism*, 98.

3. "This is love: not that we loved God, but that he loved us and sent his Son as an atoning sacrifice for our sins" (1 John 4:10).

4. "Yet to all who did receive him, to those who believed in his name, he gave the right to become children of God" (John 1:12).

THE GOD TO BE FEARED CALLS US TO HIMSELF

God calls to us through our longing to be transformed, and the God who is absolutely holy and pure offers the power to transform us!

Fourth is the phrase *that they may know you*. We long for relational intimacy. The word *know* refers not merely to intellectual knowledge but to relational intimacy. One biblical commentary says this: "Eternal life means to know experientially God and his Son, Jesus Christ."[5] Another biblical scholar even likens our relationship with God to the kind of love that the Father and the Son have in their relationship with each other: "Nor is [our] knowledge [of God] a matter simply of intellectual apprehension: it involves a personal relationship. The Father and the Son know each other in a mutuality of love, and by the knowledge of God men and women are admitted to the mystery of this divine love, being loved by God and loving him . . . in return."[6] To love someone is to know them intimately. Even more, not only do we know God, but he knows us. And when we are known by God, we are both fully known and fully accepted. As the Bible says, the Lord shares his wisdom with those who fear him: "The LORD confides in those who fear him" (Psalm 25:14).

God calls to us through our longing for relational intimacy and offers that intimacy with him for all eternity through his indwelling Holy Spirit!

In summary, God calls to us through our longings and then meets those longings through himself. We will see how he also calls to us through other means such as beauty, suffering, and the cross.

God Calls to Us Through Beauty

Think for a moment of what happens when you're listening to a beautiful symphony, walking in a majestic cathedral, hiking in the midst of a lush forest, are filled with the aroma of bread baking, are overcome by the dazzling nature of the Milky Way on a cloudless and moonless night, are taking in the sweet aroma of a rose, are holding your newborn baby for the first time, or are falling in love. Through those experiences, beauty calls out to you and transports you out of yourself and into a realm that is outside you.

English author Os Guinness writes about how beauty has a voice that calls us to itself and then uses that voice to point beyond itself:

---

5. Barton et al., *John*, 336.
6. Bruce, *Gospel of John*, 329.

> The very notion of beauty is controversial. "Beauty is impossible to define." "Beauty is in the eye of the beholder." "There is no accounting for taste...." Yet beauty is not silent. It still speaks at different levels through the beauty of art and music, the beauty of human beings, and the beauty of nature. Above all, it still speaks at times of a beauty so radiant and so attractive that it exalts, prompts, and points beyond itself to what can only be immortal, eternal, and the very source and sum of such transcendent beauty.[7]

The "voice" of beauty that Guinness talks about is supported by the fact that in the Greek language there is an etymological connection between the word for "beauty" (*kallos*) and the word for "to call" (*kalein*).[8] What that means is that beauty calls to us; it attracts us. It draws us out of ourselves and focuses us on the object of beauty.

Philosopher Roger Scruton, in his book entitled *Beauty*, writes, "Beauty makes a claim on us: it is a call to renounce our narcissism and look with reverence on the world."[9] What is narcissism? It's focusing entirely on oneself; it's declaring that I alone am of the utmost importance. It's thinking that everything revolves around me. Beauty, however, draws us out of ourselves and causes us to focus on the object of beauty that stands outside us.

I would revise Scruton's statement slightly, though. He writes that, "beauty [calls us to] look with reverence on the world." Just as a piece of art needs an artist, so, too, does the beauty in the world need an artist. Therefore, I would change his statement in this way: beauty in the world calls us to look with reverence *on the Creator* who is the source of that beauty. I agree that the world contains beauty, as Scruton said, but I would say that the world is not the source of that beauty. We should reverence—or fear—the ultimate Artist who is the source of all beauty in the world. As the source of all beauty and as the ultimate artist, God is calling us to himself through the beauty that surrounds us.

God Calls to Us Through Suffering

God also calls to us through our suffering. What does suffering do to us? It brings us to the end of ourselves. It causes us to realize how fragile we

---

7. Guinness, *Signals of Transcendence*, 113.
8. Turley, *Awakening Wonder*, ch. 3.
9. Scruton, *Beauty*, ch. 8.

are and how much we are not in control of our lives. Yes, it can cause us to lash out in anger at God and to shake our fist in his face. But suffering can also cause us to feel a sense of desperation. It is through that desperation that God calls out to us in the most powerful way. C. S. Lewis wrote, "God whispers to us in our pleasures, speaks in our conscience, but shouts in our pain: it is His megaphone to rouse a deaf world."[10] When we are desperate, we are extremely close to knowing that we are utterly dependent on God, which is one of the aspects of fearing God.

Paul wrote, "Do not be anxious about anything, but in everything, by prayer and petition, with thanksgiving, present your requests to God. And the peace of God, which transcends all understanding, will guard your hearts and your minds in Christ Jesus" (Philippians 4:6–7). Notice that Paul does not say "*for* everything," but "*in* everything." We are to be thankful and to pray not *for* everything, but we are to be thankful and to pray *in the midst of all our circumstances*, including suffering. When we do so, God will give us a peace that surpasses our understanding because we are focused on the unsurpassable and overwhelming God, which is what fearing God is all about.

God Calls to Us by Identifying with Us in Our Questioning and Doubt

Of all people, Jesus did not deserve to die. Paul wrote that "the wages of sin is death" (Romans 6:23). But that's precisely the issue. Jesus had not sinned. The author of the book of Hebrews wrote that Jesus was "tempted in every way, just as we are—yet he did not sin" (Hebrews 4:15). Jesus had lived the perfect and sinless life. What did he get for it? To be forsaken and rejected by his Father with whom he had been in a relationship of love in eternity.

Just prior to his death on the cross, Jesus cried out, "My God, my God, why have you forsaken me?" (Matthew 27:46). What was Jesus asking? He was asking what we are all inclined to ask when we're suffering: "God, don't you care? Where are you, God? Why have you abandoned me?" Are those not the first questions that enter our thoughts when we're suffering, when life doesn't make sense? That was the first question the disciples asked when their boat was about to be swamped: "Teacher, don't you care if we drown?" (Mark 4:38).

10. Lewis, *Problem of Pain*, ch. 6.

What's the significance of Jesus asking that question? It's that Jesus did not come to accuse us but to identify with us in our suffering, even to the extent of identifying with our questioning whether God cares. We often think of God as pointing his finger of blame and accusation at us for every infraction we commit. But that's simply not true. The one who accuses us is Satan. In fact, his name means "adversary" or "accuser."[11] There is a scene in the Old Testament that shows how Satan is so ready to accuse: 'Then [the angel] showed me [that is, Zechariah, the author] Joshua the high priest standing before the angel of the LORD, and Satan standing at his right side to accuse him" (Zechariah 3:1). Satan also accused Job of worshiping God only because God had blessed him with wealth: "Have you [God] not put a hedge around him and his household and everything he has? You have blessed the work of his hands, so that his flocks and herds are spread throughout the land. But stretch out your hand and strike everything he has, and he will surely curse you to your face" (Job 1:10–11). Then, too, in the book of Revelation, Satan "accuses [the believers] before our God day and night" (Revelation 12:10). Satan is still in the business of accusing us: "You are not worthy of being loved by God. Your sin is too great. What you deserve is God's condemnation, not his love. How could God possibly love a sinner like you?"

Jesus, on the other hand, did not come to accuse but to take our sins upon himself and then to pay for those sins on our behalf. Paul wrote, "God made him who had no sin to be sin for us" (2 Corinthians 5:21). As a result, God separated himself from his own Son. Why? Because Jesus had become identified with our sin, and sin is a rejection of God. Sin and God cannot coexist. The prophet Habakkuk wrote the following about God: "Your eyes are too pure to look on evil; you cannot tolerate wrongdoing" (Habakkuk 1:13).

Consider this: Jesus became so identified with us and our sin that he, like us, even questioned if God cared: "My God, my God, why have you forsaken me?" This is how much God loved us! Jesus had said, "I, when I am lifted up from the earth, will draw all people to myself" (John 12:32). John explains, "He said this to show the kind of death he was going to die" (John 12:33). By saying he would be "lifted up from the earth," Jesus was talking about his upcoming crucifixion. By being "lifted up" on the cross, Jesus draws us to himself because his death on the cross is the ultimate

---

11. Strauss, *Mark*, ch. 2.

demonstration of how much God loves and cares for us. Through the cross, God shows us his overwhelming love for us.

Even though Jesus' *feeling* of being abandoned by his Father was real—"Why have you forsaken me?"—Jesus' words of questioning whether God cares were not his most fundamental attitude. As biblical commentator D. A. Carson wrote, "Trusting God and being abandoned are not mutually exclusive."[12] Behind Jesus' words was hidden an even deeper attitude, which was a trust in the goodness and the care of God. Why do I say that? Because the words of the Old Testament always flowed so readily from Jesus' mouth, and that's what was happening here. Jesus was quoting from Psalm 22: "My God, my God, why have you forsaken me? / Why are you so far from saving me, / so far from my cries of anguish?" (Psalm 22:1). How, though, does that psalm conclude? It does so with these words of hope and trust:

> But you, Lord, do not be far from me.
>> You are my strength; come quickly to help me.
>
> Deliver me from the sword,
>> my precious life from the power of the dogs.
>
> Rescue me from the mouth of the lions;
>> save me from the horns of the wild oxen.
>
> I will declare your name to my people;
>> in the assembly I will praise you.
>
> You who fear the Lord, praise him!
>> All you descendants of Jacob, honor him!
>> Revere him, all you descendants of Israel!
>
> For he has not despised or scorned
>> the suffering of the afflicted one;
>
> he has not hidden his face from him
>> but has listened to his cry for help.
>
> (Psalm 22:19–24)

Even in the midst of despair at being abandoned by his own Father, Jesus had an unshakable trust in the life-giving power and the goodness of God. Let me remind us of the unshakable trust that Abraham had when he spoke confidently about how "we will worship and then we [both Abraham *and* Isaac] will come back to you" (Genesis 22:5). Jesus had that same

---

12. Carson, *Matthew*, "The Death of Jesus (27:45–50)."

unshakable trust when he explained "to his disciples that he must go to Jerusalem and suffer many things at the hands of the elders, the chief priests and the teachers of the law, and that he must be killed and on the third day be raised to life" (Matthew 16:21). He was predicting not only his death but also his resurrection.

Does it not move you to know that Jesus identified with us to the point of asking if God cares? Do you not feel the call of God on your heart to trust in the Savior who has come not to accuse or to condemn us, but to identify with us in our questioning and doubt?

Questions for Personal Reflection or Group Discussion

1. Do you sense that God is calling you to himself? Why or why not?
2. Of the ways that were listed that God calls us to himself—our longings (longing for eternity, longing to be made whole, longing for transformation, and longing for relational intimacy), beauty, sufferings, Jesus' identification with our questioning and doubt—which one most resonates with you?
3. Why is God calling you to himself?
4. How does God want you to respond?

12

Finding Contentment by Fearing God

ARE YOU CONTENT? IF you're like me, you're probably not sure how to answer that question because we're not clear about what it means to be content. We might have this idea that it's a vague sense of being at peace.

What I want to do in this chapter is to fill in our idea of contentment to such an extent that we realize we can't live without it, and then I also want to give us the foundation for that contentment. King Solomon, the person who wrote the book of Proverbs in the Bible, made an astonishing claim about contentment: "The fear of the LORD leads to life; then one rests content, untouched by trouble" (Proverbs 19:23). Solomon was saying that the life that comes from fearing the Lord produces a contentment that is so powerful that it allows us to face the suffering and the troubles that come our way. That's powerful stuff! That kind of contentment is something we should want to pursue. How, though, can we get to the place where we can experience that kind of contentment?

Living Under God's Authority

We're going to start our journey toward understanding contentment by looking at one of the implications of being made in the image of God. God said, "Let us make mankind in our image, in our likeness." Immediately following that statement he said, "[Let them] rule over the fish in the sea and the birds in the sky, over the livestock and all the wild animals, and over all the creatures that move along the ground" (Genesis 1:26). God creates us in his image and then immediately charges us with the responsibility of ruling over his creation. The most important aspect of that charge to rule is that we are to rule under the authority of God, not under our own authority. We are rulers in the sense that we are caretakers and stewards of his creation. Therefore, as rulers under the authority of God, we are to serve God as his ambassadors and representatives in the world.

This principle of ruling under the authority of God appears throughout the Bible. It's written in the book of Leviticus: "Do not rule over [the Israelites] ruthlessly, but fear your God" (Leviticus 25:43). King David had this to say about ruling: "When one rules over people in righteousness, when he rules in the fear of God, he is like the light of morning at sunrise on a cloudless morning, like the brightness after rain that brings grass from the earth" (2 Samuel 23:3-4). When one rules mindful that he is ruling under the authority, or the fear, of God, then his rule will be characterized as having a justice and a wisdom that are as clear, as bright, and as refreshing as the shining light of a morning sunrise following a cleansing rain.

The prophet Nehemiah, who was tasked with rebuilding the wall around Jerusalem, wrote, "The earlier governors—those preceding me—placed a heavy burden on the people and took forty shekels of silver from them in addition to food and wine. Their assistants also lorded it over the people. *But out of reverence [fear] for God I did not act like that*" (Nehemiah 5:15, emphasis added).

Even our relationships with each other are to be under the authority of God. As Paul wrote, "Submit to one another out of reverence [fear] for Christ" (Ephesians 5:21).

Jesus is our ultimate example of living under the authority and the rule of God his Father. We see that in these words: "Very truly I [Jesus] tell you, the Son can do nothing by himself; he can do only what he sees his Father doing, because whatever the Father does the Son also does" (John 5:19). Do Jesus' words surprise you? We need to remember that he was speaking as the God who had become an incarnate man and was therefore giving us the prime example of how we are to live in utter dependence on and under the authority and rule of God.

I'll Give You All the Kingdoms of the World

What do we think about living under the authority and rule of God? Do we not bristle at the thought of living under the authority and rule of anyone, including God? We want to call the shots. We want to be in control of our own lives. We resonate with the defiant words that William Ernest Henley (1849–1903) wrote in his poem "Invictus": "I am the master of my fate, / I am the captain of my soul."[1] The word *invictus* is Latin for "unconquered, unsubdued, invincible."[2]

With Jesus, though, we never detect any sense that he felt discontented living under the authority of God. In fact, he found complete and total satisfaction doing the will of his Father. He said, "I love the Father and . . . I do exactly what my Father has commanded me" (John 14:31). He even goes so far as to compare doing the will of God to the sustaining, life-giving, fulfilling, and nourishing power of food: "My food is to do the will of him who sent me" (John 4:34).

Where, though, do we see someone in the Bible who is discontented about living under God's authority and rule? We see it in Satan. In the following encounter between Satan and Jesus, we see how Satan is discontented with his lot in life, and he wants more: "The devil took him [Jesus] to a very high mountain and showed him all the kingdoms of the world and their splendor. 'All this I will give you,' he said, 'if you will bow down and worship me'" (Matthew 4:8–9). Why did Satan tempt Jesus in the way that he did? He knew full well who Jesus was. He knew Jesus had created all things, and as the Creator, he alone deserved to be worshiped, not Satan. So, what exactly did Satan hope to gain by tempting Jesus to worship him? The answer is freedom, independence, and absolute autonomy from God. Satan was blaming Jesus, as his Creator, for holding him back. He was thinking, "If Jesus would worship me, then I would be greater than him and would be free to be all I can be. No restrictions! No limitations!" Jesus, Satan thought, was holding him back from realizing his full, albeit evil, potential.

Satan's attitude was the complete opposite of Jesus' attitude. Jesus was content living under the authority and rule of God. To Satan, though, living under God's authority was oppressive, limiting, and restrictive. He was anything but content living under God's authority and rule. As John Milton's Satan said after being banished from heaven, "Better to reign in Hell than serve in Heaven."[3]

Where do you stand when it comes to living under God's authority and rule? Who best represents your perspective? Jesus or Satan?

1. Jenson, "Invictus."
2. Jenson, "Invictus."
3. Milton, *Paradise Lost*, book 1, line 263.

PART II: *DISCOVERING ONE'S TRUE SELF*

The Ambassador Who Chose to Represent Himself

How can we make a case for how living under God's authority and rule brings contentment? Imagine this scenario: You're the ambassador who represents the most powerful country in the world. As you live in the country to which you have been assigned as ambassador, you enjoy all the rights and privileges of that position. You're given great honor and respect. People listen to what you have to say because you speak for your president and your country. Your word has weight, and you have value.

After several years of serving your country as ambassador with great loyalty, though, you decide to represent your own views and not those of your president and your country. You justify your decision by saying that you have been feeling devalued and insignificant by having to serve only as a mouthpiece for someone else. You are more than a mouthpiece! You are you, and you have value just being who you are. You don't need to represent anyone else to have value. Plus, your word has just as much validity and weight as those of your president. It's about time people recognize that you have value simply for being you and also recognize the value of your words.

What would happen to you as an ambassador if you decided to represent only yourself and not your country? You would lose your value as an ambassador, and your words would no longer carry any weight. You had value and your words had weight only because you represented the president and the country for which you were an ambassador.

The above scenario is not hypothetical; it actually happened. On March 4, 2025, Phil Goff, New Zealand's high commissioner to the United Kingdom, publicly asked a question of Finland's Foreign Minister Elina Valtonen that disparaged the wisdom and the historical knowledge of President Trump, insinuating that the president's actions toward Russian President Vladimir Putin were like those of Britain's Prime Minister Neville Chamberlain toward Adolf Hitler. Goff was dismissed from his position and sent back to New Zealand. New Zealand's Foreign Minister Winston Peters said, "When you are in that position you represent the government and the policies of the day. You're not able to free think, you are the face of New Zealand." Apparently, Goff had forgotten that he was in the UK to represent New Zealand and not his own personal opinions.[4]

---

4. Graham-McLay, "New Zealand's Top Diplomat." Thanks to Dr. Darrell Dooyema for alerting me to this article.

Having made us in his image, we are ambassadors or representative of God. We have value and authority and purpose only as we live as his representatives to the world. We don't see it that way, though, do we? We think that we have value in and of ourselves. We are our own authority. We don't need to live under the authority and rule of God. Take the thinking that is common today called "expressive individualism." Expressive individualism is very much like the ambassador who declared that he will represent only himself, not his country. Through the mentality of expressive individualism, we have severed ourselves from being made in God's image and living under his authority and rule (mimesis) and have chosen instead to define who we are in our true selves and to live under our own authority (poiesis). If expressive individualism is true, then "the individual is king, [and he] can be whoever he wants to be."[5] Our highest goal, we believe, is to be true to ourselves. It's to live authentic lives, whether or not our lives conform to the morals and customs imposed on us by our surrounding culture. If expressive individualism is our way of thinking, then it is therefore appropriate to say that we have indeed become ambassadors representing only ourselves.

Does expressive individualism lead to contentment? Does it bring a sense of satisfaction? Does it fill one's life with peace? Does it give us the kind of equanimity that allows us to face all the troubles in life that might come our way?

Expressive individualism teaches us to place the rights and power of the individual to define oneself in ways that are often in opposition to the surrounding culture. Carl Trueman, in his book *The Rise and Triumph of the Modern Self*, writes, "Satisfaction and meaning—authenticity—are now found by an inward turn, and the culture is reconfigured to this end. Indeed, it must now serve the purpose of meeting my psychological needs; I must not tailor my psychological needs to the nature of society, for that would create anxiety and make me inauthentic."[6]

Still, though, even though we, through expressive individualism, have focused on the power of the individual to define their own identities and to be true to themselves, we can never escape living in a context that is social. Trueman wrote, "Expressive individualism is a social phenomenon that emerges through the dialogical nature of what it means to be a person. As [sociologist Charles Taylor] expresses it, 'One is a self only among other selves. A self can never be described without reference to

---

5. Trueman, *Rise and Triumph*, 50.
6. Trueman, *Rise and Triumph*, 54.

those who surround it."⁷ This means that my sense of whether or not I have value is largely dependent on how others view me. Again, Trueman writes, "Identity... arises in the context of belonging. To have an identity means that I am being acknowledged by others. To wander through a town and to be ignored by everyone I encounter would understandably lead me to question whether they considered me to be a nonperson or at least a person unworthy of acknowledgment. If I am treated by everyone I encounter as if I am worthless, I will probably end up feeling that I am worthless."⁸ If our contentment—or, as Trueman writes, our sense of "satisfaction and meaning [and] authenticity"—is based on others in the culture meeting our psychological needs by affirming our declared identity, then it is based on shaky grounds indeed. Obviously, we do value what other people think of us, but that can't be the source of and the foundation for our contentment. Our contentment must be based on something much more solid, enduring, and dependable. The idea that we can define ourselves, however, does not provide such a solid, enduring, and dependable foundation. If we are the ones who define ourselves, then we can also change our minds as to who we are.

The only solid, enduring, and dependable foundation for our contentment is realizing that we have been made in the image of God and that we are his representatives living under his authority and rule. That's exactly what Jesus meant when he said, "The Son can do nothing by himself." Since God made us in his image, we can rest assured that we have an unshakable foundation for our value and significance because we were made not only to reflect his image but also to represent him in the world.

Contentment Comes from Fearing God

Jesus was content living under the authority and rule of God. And, if I am correct that we can learn about the fear of God from verses that don't mention the word "fear," then his contentment came from fearing God. I say that because all three aspects of what it looks like to fear God are found in the verse "The Son can do nothing by himself; he can do only what he sees his Father doing, because whatever the Father does the Son also does" (John 5:19). Jesus is saying that he lives in *utter dependence* on the Father ("can do nothing by himself"), gives God his *undivided attention* ("can do

---

7. Trueman, *Rise and Triumph*, 57.
8. Trueman, *Rise and Triumph*, 57–58.

only what he sees his father doing"), and has an *unshakable trust* in him ("whatever the Father does the Son also does").

I Can Do Everything

Paul, too, talked about being content: "I have learned to be content whatever the circumstances. I know what it is to be in need, and I know what it is to have plenty. I have learned the secret of being content in any and every situation, whether well fed or hungry, whether living in plenty or in want. I can do everything through him who gives me strength" (Philippians 4:11–13). What did Paul mean by *everything* in the phrase "I can do everything"? Was he referring to a power-of-positive-thinking attitude where if you believe it, you can achieve it? No. Paul was talking simply about being content no matter what life threw at him, whether being hungry or well-fed, being in need or having plenty. Paul elaborated on what he means by Christ giving him strength ("through him who gives me strength") when he wrote,

> What is more, I consider everything a loss because of the surpassing worth of knowing Christ Jesus my Lord, for whose sake I have lost all things. I consider them garbage, that I may gain Christ and be found in him, not having a righteousness of my own that comes from the law, but that which is through faith in Christ—the righteousness that comes from God on the basis of faith. (Philippians 3:8–9)

Again, as we saw with the words of Jesus, the three aspects of fearing God appear in the way Paul talks about his faith in Christ. Through the words "I consider everything a loss," Paul was declaring his *utter dependence* on what Christ has done on his behalf. He was not trusting at all in his own merit. Through the words "the surpassing worth of knowing Christ Jesus my Lord," Paul was saying that his greatest desire is to be in a relationship with Christ, which is to give Christ his *undivided attention*. Finally, through the words "not having a righteousness of my own that comes from the law, but that which is through faith in Christ," Paul was declaring his *unshakable trust* in the work of Jesus Christ to be made right with God.

The implications of what Paul has done in Philippians 3:8–9 are huge. They can't be overstated. Let me explain. We've been talking all throughout this book about the fear of God. In a sense, God has been this distant, transcendent, unapproachable being who is "out there." By applying the three aspects of fearing God to Jesus, though, Paul is saying that fearing Christ is the same as fearing God, except that fearing Christ makes fearing God much more up close and personal. Not only is Jesus the God who has made himself known to us, but he also enters our lives and indwells us through the Holy Spirit as we place our faith in Jesus. He can do this because, as Paul wrote, "the Lord . . . is the Spirit" (2 Corinthians 3:18).

Paul not only applies the three aspects of what it looks like to fear God to Jesus, but we see that he also applies the fact that we are to worship God alone to Jesus. After Paul talks about how Jesus was "obedient to death—even death on a cross" (Philippians 2:8), he says, "Therefore God exalted him to the highest place and gave him the name that is above every name, that at the name of Jesus every knee should bow, in heaven and on earth and under the earth, and every tongue confess that Jesus Christ is Lord, to the glory of God the Father" (Philippians 2:9–11). Jesus is worthy of our worship and of our fear!

A Peace That Transcends Understanding

How is this related to the main topic of this chapter—finding contentment? Paul wrote, "I can do everything through him [Jesus] who gives me strength (Philippians 4:11–13). As we've already discussed, what Paul meant by *everything* was the ability to be content no matter what circumstances he faced. The verse says that Jesus gave him the strength to face troubles and to find contentment. How, though, did Paul tap into the strength that Jesus gives? He did so through prayer: "Do not be anxious about anything, but in everything, by prayer and petition, with thanksgiving, present your requests to God. And the peace of God, which transcends all understanding, will guard your hearts and your minds in Christ Jesus" (Philippians 4:6–7). That "peace of God, which transcends all understanding," is the contentment that Paul was talking about. Consider the wisdom in these words from Thomas Watson (1620–1686), an English Puritan preacher: "Prayer . . . is the unburdening of the soul, the unloading of all our cares into God's hands, and this ushers in sweet contentment. When there is any burden on our spirit, opening up to a friend [such as Jesus] eases and quiets our heart. It is not our strong resolutions, but our strong requests to God, which gives the heart ease in suffering. Through prayer, the strength of Christ is brought into the soul. And when that exists, a man is able to go through any condition."[9]

9. Watson and Roth, *Art of Divine Contentment*, ch. 9, rule 18.

Why, though, did Paul describe the peace in the way that he did—as "the peace of God, which transcends all understanding"? We correctly associate "transcends all understanding" with our having a sense of peace, but the reason that the peace we experience can be beyond our understanding is because it's based on the God who is beyond our understanding, is beyond our fathoming, and is to be feared.

Even more, "the peace of God [that] transcends all understanding" is based on the unfathomable nature of what God has done for us through his Son, Jesus Christ. The author of the book of Hebrews wrote, "Keep your lives free from the love of money and be content with what you have, because God has said, 'Never will I leave you; never will I forsake you'" (Hebrews 13:5). The statement, "Never will I leave you; never will I forsake you," is easy enough to understand. When you think about its implications, though, it's unfathomable. God will never, ever leave us! God will be with us for all eternity! That is beyond our understanding. Everyone we know eventually leaves us when they die. That's the reality we're used to. That's the norm. As much as we hate it, we've come to expect it. But that's not true of God. He will never, ever leave us. *Never, ever, for all eternity!*

What is even more amazing is that he will never forsake us. Why will he never forsake us? Because he cannot forsake his own Son Jesus Christ. He can never forsake us because as we place our faith and trust in Jesus, we are then identified with him. If God were to forsake us who are "in Christ," it would be like forsaking himself. That's the implication of the doctrine of the Trinity. Being "in Christ" does not mean that we become Christ. We are not one with Christ in regard to his being, but we are one with him relationally. When we place our faith in Christ, we become identified with Christ. We become part of his family. We become his child. We are adopted into his family. We are also married to Christ. His identity is now our identity. His name is written on our foreheads. And since we are "in Christ," it would be just as impossible for God to forsake us as it would be for him to forsake his very own Son. Puritan preacher Thomas Watson wrote, "A contented Christian is like Noah in the ark; although he was tossed by the waves, Noah could sit and sing in the ark."[10] Being "in Christ" is a much greater place of security than even the ark. The truth of our being identified with and therefore secure in Christ is unfathomable.

---

10. Watson and Roth, *Art of Divine Contentment*, ch. 6. See the section titled "The Excellency of Contentment."

That identification with Christ is the foundation for and the source of our contentment. We can face whatever suffering or troubles come our way because they do not attack who we are, which is our core identity of being "in Christ." Who we are—our core identity, our true self, our most authentic image—is secure in our being identified with Christ. Citing Thomas Watson again, "[An] argument or motive for contentment is that we already have everything that should make us content. Has God not given us Christ? In him there are 'unsearchable riches' (Eph. 3:8). . . . Why do you need to complain of the world's emptiness, when you have God's fullness?"[11] What did Watson mean by "fullness"? He meant our being identified with Christ: "For in Christ all the fullness of the Deity lives in bodily form, and in Christ you have been brought to fullness" (Colossians 2:9–10). And Jesus said, "I have come that they may have life, and have it to the full" (John 10:10).

Fearing God Means Fearing Christ

As we fear God, we should also fear Christ. As we fear Christ, we will realize that we are *utterly dependent* on Christ for our existence and for being made in God's image; we will give him our *undivided attention* as we are fully in love with him; and we will rest in the *unshakable trust* that we have in what he has done for us by dying on our behalf for our sins and then rising from the dead so that we, too, can have that resurrection life.

What does that unshakable trust in Christ gain us? Paul wrote, "When you believed, you were marked in him with a seal, the promised Holy Spirit, who is a deposit guaranteeing our inheritance until the redemption of those who are God's possession—to the praise of his glory" (Ephesians 1:13–14). Notice the terms in those two verses that indicate something that is certain: seal, promise, deposit guaranteeing, possession. Those words of certainty should give us a great sense of contentment. Our future is certain. Nothing can shake it. And all of that is based merely on our placing our faith and trust in Christ. It's a gift we receive by faith, not based on our merit: "For it is by grace you have been saved, through faith—and this not from yourselves, it is the gift of God—not by works, so that no one can boast" (Ephesians 2:8–9). If salvation were based on our efforts, then it would not be certain. But because it's based on what the all-powerful God

---

11. Watson and Roth, *Art of Divine Contentment*, ch. 6. See the section titled "The Riches of the Believer."

FINDING CONTENTMENT BY FEARING GOD

has done on our behalf, then it can be certain. Again, there should be great contentment in knowing we are safe in the hands of God.

The Image of God and Our True Self

Part of the purpose of this book is to talk about our true self, our core identity. Who are we? What is our true self? Our true self is that we were made in the image of God. To know what it means to be made in the image of God, we need only to look to Jesus. Paul wrote of "Christ, who is the image of God" (2 Corinthians 4:4) and said, "The Son [Jesus] is the image of the invisible God" (Colossians 1:15). Jesus, of whom the Bible says, "Through him all things were made; without him nothing was made that has been made" (John 1:3), was there at the beginning making us in his image.

The most important aspect of having been made in the image of God—our true self—is that we were made to fear God, which is the knowledge that God alone is God; to be overwhelmed in our passion for him; to live in utter dependence on him; to give him our undivided attention; and to have an unshakable trust in him. Fearing God is what we were made for. It's what will most fulfill us.

What it means to have Christ's name written on the believer's forehead, as it says in Revelation, is that Christ has revived—given new life to—our ability to live according to that image. As the Creator and as the one who was also fully man, Jesus has the transforming and creative power through the indwelling Holy Spirit to bring life to our ability to live according to the original true self in which we were made, which is the image of God. We can rest content in knowing who we are as having been made in the image of God and knowing that the Holy Spirit gives us the power to live according to that image.

Questions for Personal Reflection or Group Discussion

1. What do you think of the idea of living under the authority and rule of God? How do you feel about that?
2. What do you think of the ambassador analogy? Do you think it accurately communicates how we have value and significance only as we represent and live under the rule of God?

PART II: *DISCOVERING* ONE'S TRUE SELF

3. What does being content mean to you? How important is it to be content?

4. How does being identified with Christ, which means being "in Christ," bring contentment to you?

5. What is our true self, our core identity?

Concluding Thoughts

13

Utter Dependence Is the Foundation for Fearing God

In our journey toward understanding what it means to fear God, a recurring theme has appeared. The theme of *utter dependence*. Of course, utter dependence is the first aspect of what it looks like to fear God. We realize that we are utterly dependent on God for our existence, not only because he created us out of nothing but also because he sustains us every moment of every day.

Then, too, with each of the other two aspects of what it looks like to fear God, utter dependence is part of them as well. Utter dependence helps us give God our undivided attention. We used the analogy of the scuba diver who, because he was utterly dependent on the breathing apparatus, was aware of the presence of that breathing apparatus at all times. In the same way, because we are aware of God sustaining us in our existence at all times, there is a part of our consciousness that is giving God our undivided attention. Each breath we take should remind us that God is sustaining us.

Then, too, utter dependence was part of our having an unshakable trust in God. When we talked about Abraham, we looked at the verse in Hebrews where it says, "By faith Abraham, when God tested him, offered Isaac as a sacrifice. He who had embraced the promises was about to sacrifice his one and only son, even though God had said to him, 'It is through Isaac that your offspring will be reckoned.' Abraham reasoned that God could even raise the dead" (Hebrews 11:17–19). Why could God raise the dead? Because he has life in himself. And because God is the one who gives

UTTER DEPENDENCE IS THE FOUNDATION FOR FEARING GOD

all things life, we are utterly dependent on him. Abraham's utter dependence on God as the Creator caused him to have an unshakable trust in God to be able to somehow fulfill his promise to Abraham through Isaac, even though he had asked Abraham to sacrifice Isaac.

When we looked at how we are to have the same attitude as Jesus in regard to living for the interests of others, part of Jesus' motivation for having that attitude was utter dependence. By "emptying himself" and temporarily suspending the use of some of his divine attributes, Jesus lived in utter dependence on his Father. For Jesus, utter dependence on the Father was not oppressive; it was life.

Utter dependence also gives humanity a powerful motivation for unity. It grabs our attention, moves us, and even has the power to transform us. The realization that we are each utterly dependent on God for our existence should shock us into a sense of humility, stop our boasting, and help us see that we are nothing apart from the God who gives us life.

Utter dependence is also relevant when it comes to our ability to forgive. Because forgiveness is so hard, we're utterly dependent on the power of the Holy Spirit to change our hearts and to remind us of how we have been forgiven through Jesus Christ.

Then, finally, we saw how, as ambassadors and representatives living under the authority and rule of God, we are utterly dependent on him for our value and significance.

Weakness Is an Advantage

In light of how utter dependence has been the underlying theme of fearing God, consider these words by author J. D. Greear about dependence and weakness, which I found to be profound:

> When God makes you weak, it's not because he has forgotten you. Quite the opposite. He is inviting you to lean into the power of his Spirit. And that's the greatest invitation you'll ever receive.
>
> Dependence, not strength, is God's objective for you. *And if dependence is the objective, then weakness is an advantage.*
>
> *Your* strength is likely your greatest impediment [to leaning into the power of his Spirit]. So rejoice when God makes you weak. He does so in order that you can become strong in his Spirit.

Sometimes he puts you flat on your back so you will finally be looking in the right direction.[1]

That entire quote is worth reading again, but I want to focus on two of the sentences: "*Dependence, not strength, is God's objective for you. And if* [utter] *dependence is the objective, then weakness becomes an advantage.*"

Is utter dependence on God really his objective for us? Does weakness give us an advantage? Those questions are the key questions of this book. They are the questions that underlie all that we have talked about. Those questions get at the heart of how we see ourselves, do they not? Our natural response is to say, "Absolutely not! Independence, not dependence, is the objective. Self-expression is the objective. The objective is asserting my right to define for myself who I am, to express that true self, and to demand that the culture both affirm and celebrate my choices. That is what will bring me fulfillment. That is what will allow me to live authentically. Weakness and dependence have no part of it."

So why would dependence be God's objective for us? Why is weakness a strength when it comes to our relationship with God? Because our being utterly dependent on God is the way things are. It's the truth. It's reality. Such utter dependence is not subservience, however. It's anything but subservience. It's life-giving. It's the way God made us. He created us from nothing so that we could experience overwhelming fulfillment being in a relationship of love with the infinite, loving, dangerous God. Utter dependence on God is our purpose in life. It's the way we were meant to be. Utter dependence on God is our home, the place where we belong.

To help us understand what I'm saying, I want to revisit the scuba diver analogy again, only this time I want to apply the attribute of personal consciousness and awareness to the breathing apparatus. As such, the breathing apparatus actually enjoys supplying its life-giving air to the diver because it cares for her. It gives her air knowing that, as it does so, she is then able to be fulfilled by enjoying the thrill of exploring the wonders of the ocean. And her dependence on that breathing apparatus is the truth of how things are. It's reality. Suppose she were to say to the breathing apparatus, "I don't want to be dependent on you anymore. My dependence on you is limiting, restrictive. I want to be independent. I want to be free from you. I want to be free to be who I want to be; I want my freedom, my independence!" As a result, she rips off the scuba gear. The inevitable result is obvious.

---

1. Greear, *Jesus, Continued*, 221; emphasis in original.

UTTER DEPENDENCE IS THE FOUNDATION FOR FEARING GOD

As noted above, Greear wrote, "[God] is inviting you to lean into the power of his Spirit. And that's the greatest invitation you'll ever receive." There's a connection between the power of the Holy Spirit and the scuba diving analogy. The connection is that the Hebrew word *ruach*, which is often used in the Bible to refer to the Holy Spirit, can be translated either as "breath" or "spirit." In a sense, both are true when it comes to the Holy Spirit. The Holy Spirit is the breathing apparatus in the life of the believer because he breathes life into our dead souls so that we can be in a relationship with God. The Holy Spirit is the one who gives us the very same resurrection life that raised Jesus from the dead: "If [or since] the Spirit of him who raised Jesus from the dead is living in you, he who raised Christ from the dead will also give life to your mortal bodies through his Spirit, who lives in you" (Romans 8:11). The Holy Spirit is the one who gives us the power to be in Christ, and as we are "in Christ, the new creation has come [we are the new creation]: The old has gone, the new is here!" (2 Corinthians 5:17). The Holy Spirit is the one who causes us to be born again, which means being born into God's family. Jesus said, "Very truly I tell you, no one can see the kingdom of God unless they are born again. . . . No one can enter the kingdom of God unless they are born of water and the Spirit. Flesh gives birth to flesh, but the Spirit gives birth to spirit (John 3:3, 5–6), and also "to all who did receive him, to those who believed in his name, he gave the right to become children of God—children born not of natural descent, nor of human decision or a husband's will, but born of God" (John 1:12-13). The Holy Spirit is the one who is the living water that wells up to eternal life. Jesus told the Samaritan woman, "Everyone who drinks this water [from the well] will be thirsty again, but whoever drinks the water I give them will never thirst. Indeed, the water I give them will become in them a spring of water welling up to eternal life" (John 4:13-14). The Holy Spirit helps us in our weakness when we don't know how to pray for something or someone: "The Spirit helps us in our weakness. We do not know what we ought to pray for, but the Spirit himself intercedes for us through wordless groans" (Romans 8:26). The Holy Spirit does all of this as we place our faith and trust in Jesus as the one who paid the price for our sins in full.

Rather than fighting and resisting God, fear him. Realize that you are *utterly dependent* on him and that your weakness is your strength. Jesus is calling you to himself through these words: "Come to me, all you who are weary and burdened, and I will give you rest" (Matthew 11:28). You can experience that rest as you declare your utter dependence on him, and in that rest, you will find overwhelming fulfillment. Give him your *undivided attention* as one who is so enamored by the beauty of God that to be attracted to anything or anyone less would be settling for less than who you were made to be. And live with an *unshakable trust* in God's goodness and care even when life doesn't make sense. The Bible says, "The LORD delights in those who fear him, / who put their hope in his unfailing love" (Psalm 147:11).

Questions for Personal Reflection or Group Discussion

1. Consider the sentence, "If [utter] dependence is the objective, then weakness becomes an advantage." What does that sentence mean?
2. Does the sentence above resonate with you? Why or why not?
3. What are your thoughts about the connection between the analogy of the breathing apparatus in scuba diving and the Holy Spirit breathing life into the life of the believer?
4. How have your ideas of what it means to fear God changed over the course of reading this book?
5. Do you now see a place for fearing God in your life? Why or why not?

Bibliography

Augustine, Saint. *Confessions*. Translated by R. S. Pine-Coffin. New York: Penguin, 1961. Kindle.

Barna, George. *New Insights into the Generation of Growing Influence: Millennials in America*. Glendale, AZ: Cultural Research Center at Arizona Christian University, 2021.

Barrett, Matthew. *None Greater: The Undomesticated Attributes of God*. Grand Rapids: Baker, 2019.

Barton, Bruce, et al. *Life Application Bible Commentary: John*. Edited by Grant Osborne. Carol Stream, IL: Tyndale House, 1993.

Barton, Bruce, et al. *Life Application Bible Commentary: Luke*. Edited by Grant Osborne. Wheaton, IL: Tyndale House, 1997.

Barton, Bruce, et al. *Life Application Bible Commentary: Philippians, Colossians, and Philemon*. Edited by Grant Osborne. Carol Stream, IL: Tyndale House, 1995.

Beale, G. K. *We Become What We Worship: A Biblical Theology of Idolatry*. Downers Grove, IL: IVP Academic, 2008.

Beale, G. K., and David Campbell. *Revelation: A Shorter Commentary*. Grand Rapids: Eerdmans, 2015. Kindle.

Benner, David. *The Gift of Being Yourself: The Sacred Call to Self-Discovery*. Downers Grove, IL: InterVarsity, 2004.

Blomberg, Craig. *The NIV Application Commentary: 1 Corinthians*. Grand Rapids: Zondervan, 1994.

Boa, Kenneth, and Robert Bowman Jr. *20 Compelling Evidences That God Exists: Discover Why Believing in God Makes So Much Sense*. Colorado Springs, CO: Cook, 2005. Kindle.

Bradbury, Ray. "The Up Side." *Guideposts* 56.4 (2001) 9.

Brooks, Arthur. *Love Your Enemies: How Decent People Can Save America from the Culture of Contempt*. New York: Broadside, 2019.

Brother Lawrence. *The Practice of the Presence of God*. New Kensington, PA: Whitaker, 1982. Kindle.

BIBLIOGRAPHY

Bruce, F. F. *The Gospel of John: Introduction, Exposition and Notes*. Grand Rapids: Eerdmans, 1983.

Byrd, Richard. *Alone*. New York: Kodansha International, 1938.

Carson, D. A. *Matthew: The Expositor's Bible Commentary*. Rev. ed. Edited by Tremper Longman III and David E. Garland. Grand Rapids: Zondervan, 2010. Kindle.

Cheaney, Janie B. "The Things They Carry: Identity Is Too Heavy a Weight for Children to Bear Alone." *World* 38.11 (2023) 42.

Churchland, Patricia. *Neurophilosophy: Toward a Unified Science of the Mind/Brain*. Cambridge, MA: MIT, 1986.

Collins, Francis. *The Language of God: A Scientist Presents Evidence for Belief*. New York: Free Press, 2006.

Copan, Paul, and William Lane Craig. *Creation out of Nothing: A Biblical, Philosophical, and Scientific Exploration*. Grand Rapids: Baker Academic; Leicester: Apollos, 2004.

Craig, William Lane. *On Guard: Defending Your Faith with Reason and Precision*. Colorado Springs, CO: Cook, 2010.

Dembski, William, et al., eds. *The Comprehensive Guide to Science and Faith*. Eugene, OR: Harvest House, 2021.

Denton, Michael. *Evolution: A Theory in Crisis*. Bethesda, MD: Adler & Adler, 1986.

Dyck, Drew. *Yawning at Tigers: You Can't Tame God, So Stop Trying*. Nashville: Nelson, 2014.

Eldredge, John. *Dare to Desire: An Invitation to Fulfill Your Deepest Dreams*. Nashville: J. Countryman, 2002.

Faber, Frederick William. *Faber's Hymns*. New York: Crowell, 1894.

Frankl, Viktor. *Man's Search for Meaning*. New York: Washington Square, 1984.

Galli, Mark. "The Fear That Draws Us." *Christianity Today* 57.9 (2013) 46–49.

Ganssle, Gregory. *Thinking About God*. Downers Grove, IL: IVP Academic, 2004.

Geisler, Norman. *God, Creation*. Vol. 2 of *Systematic Theology*. Minneapolis: Bethany House, 2003.

Geisler, Norman, and Frank Turek. *I Don't Have Enough Faith to Be an Atheist*. Wheaton, IL: Crossway, 2004.

Graham-McLay, Charlotte. "New Zealand's Top Diplomat in London Loses His Job over Remarks About Trump." Associated Press, last updated Mar. 6, 2025. https://apnews.com/article/trump-goff-zealand-uk-diplomat-chatham-london-3c3a55e5b45170da815f76ff5873ab70.

Greear, J. D. *Jesus, Continued: Why the Spirit Inside You Is Better than the Jesus Beside You*. Grand Rapids: Zondervan, 2014.

Groothuis, Douglas. *Christian Apologetics: A Comprehensive Case for Biblical Faith*. 2nd ed. Downers Grove, IL: IVP Academic, 2022.

Guinness, Os. *Signals of Transcendence: Listening to the Promptings of Life*. Downers Grove, IL: InterVarsity, 2023.

Halverson, Keith (keiths.creations). "I am my own religion." Instagram, Feb. 7, 2023.

———. "I shall rise today." Instagram, Feb. 10, 2023.

———. "My heart does burst with blessings." Instagram, May 17, 2023.

———. "There is no higher purpose." Instagram, May 22, 2023.

Hoekema, Anthony. *Created in God's Image*. Grand Rapids: Eerdmans, 1986.

Horner, Grant. *Meaning at the Movies: Becoming a Discerning Viewer*. Wheaton, IL: Crossway, 2010.

BIBLIOGRAPHY

Jackson, Peter, dir. *The Lord of the Rings: The Two Towers*. Burbank, CA: New Line Cinemas, 2002.

Jenson, Jamie. "Invictus by William Ernest Henley." Poem Analysis, Mar. 6, 2023. https://poemanalysis.com/william-ernest-henley/invictus/.

Kalanithi, Paul. *When Breath Becomes Air*. New York: Random House, 2016. Kindle.

Keller, Timothy, and Kathy Keller. *The Meaning of Marriage: Facing the Complexities of Commitment with the Wisdom of God*. New York: Penguin, 2016.

King, Martin Luther, Jr. *A Testament of Hope: The Essential Writings and Speeches*. Edited by James M. Washington. New York: HarperOne, 1991.

Lamont, Corliss. *The Philosophy of Humanism*. New York: Continuum, 1988.

Levi, Allen. *The Last Sweet Mile: A Journey of Brothers*. Cane Ridge, TN: Rabbit Room, 2015. Kindle.

Lewis, C. S. *Mere Christianity*. New York: HarperSanFrancisco, 1980.

———. *The Problem of Pain*. New York: HarperCollins, 1996.

———. *The Weight of Glory and Other Addresses*. Grand Rapids: Eerdmans, 1979.

Lightfoot, J. B. *St. Paul's Epistle to the Philippians*. Grand Rapids: Zondervan, 1953.

MacArthur, John. *The MacArthur New Testament Commentary: Matthew 8–15*. Chicago: Moody, 1987. Kindle.

Magnuson, Ed. "They Slipped the Surly Bonds of Earth to Touch the Face of God." *Time* (Feb. 10, 1986) 24–37.

Mandela, Nelson. *Long Walk to Freedom: The Autobiography of Nelson Mandela*. With a foreword by President Bill Clinton. New York: Little, Brown, 2008. Kindle.

Martin, Albert. *The Forgotten Fear: Where Have All the God-Fearers Gone?* Grand Rapids: Reformation Heritage, 2015. Kindle.

Metaxas, Eric. *Fish out of Water: A Search for the Meaning of Life*. Washington, DC: Salem, 2021. Kindle.

Meyer, Stephen. *Return of the God Hypothesis: Three Scientific Discoveries That Reveal the Mind Behind the Universe*. New York: HarperOne, 2021.

———. *Signature in the Cell: DNA and Evidence for Intelligent Design*. New York: HarperOne, 2009.

Milton, John. *Paradise Lost*. In *The Norton Anthology of English Literature*, rev. ed., vol. 1, edited by M. H. Abrams, 1036–1141. New York: Norton, 1968.

Motyer, J. Alex. *The Prophecy of Isaiah: An Introduction and Commentary*. Downers Grove, IL: InterVarsity, 1993.

Murphy, Denis Liam. *The Blame Game: How to Recover from the World's Oldest Addiction*. New York: Post Hill, 2023. Kindle.

Noble, Alan. *You Are Not Your Own: Belonging to God in an Inhuman World*. Downers Grove, IL: InterVarsity, 2021. Kindle.

Parkison, Samuel. *To Gaze upon God: The Beatific Vision in Doctrine, Tradition, and Practice*. Downers Grove, IL: IVP Academic, 2024. Kindle.

Parnell, Jonathan. "Church Discipline and Expressive Individualism." *9Marks* (Mar. 2022). Kindle.

Pascal, Blaise. *Pensées*. Translated by A. J. Krailsheimer. New York: Penguin, 1966.

Pearcey, Nancy. "Phillip Johnson Was Right: The Unhappy Evolution of Darwinism." *World* 16.7 (Feb. 24, 2001). https://wng.org/articles/phillip-johnson-was-right-1617340221.

BIBLIOGRAPHY

Pereira, Yosely, and Bill Ivey. *A Sea Between Us: The True Story of a Man Who Risked Everything for Family and Freedom.* Carol Stream, IL: Tyndale Momentum, 2022. Kindle.

Perry, Matthew. *Friends, Lovers, and the Big Terrible Thing: A Memoir.* New York: Flatiron, 2022. Kindle.

Pieper, Josef. *Leisure: The Basis of Culture.* Translated by Alexander Dru. San Francisco: Ignatius, 1952. Kindle.

Piper, John. *The Legacy of Sovereign Joy: God's Triumphant Grace in the Lives of Augustine, Luther, and Calvin.* Wheaton, IL: Crossway, 2000.

Popova, Maria. "The Thing in Itself: C. S. Lewis on What We Long for in Our Existential Longing." Marginalian, Sept. 3, 2022. https://www.themarginalian.org/2022/09/03/c-s-lewis-longing/?mc_cid=1447853901&mc_eid=7ffdbd2841.

Ramirez, Michael. "Our Moral Compass." Cartoon in *Gazette* (CO), Dec. 12, 2023.

Revell, Anna. *Apartheid: A History of Apartheid.* Self published, 2017. Kindle.

Sagan, Carl. *Broca's Brain: Reflections on the Romance of Science.* New York: Random House, 1974.

Sanger, Larry. "How a Skeptical Philosopher Becomes a Christian." Larrysanger.org, Feb. 5, 2025. https://larrysanger.org/2025/02/how-a-skeptical-philosopher-becomes-a-christian/.

Scheinin, Richard. "Father's death sends Deepak Chopra back to the basics." *Milwaukee Journal Sentinel* (WI), Apr. 15, 2001.

Scruton, Roger. *Beauty.* New York: Oxford University Press, 2009.

Smalts, Laura Perry. *Transgender to Transformed: A Story of Transition That Will Truly Set You Free.* Bartlesville, OK: Genesis Publishing Group, 2019. Kindle.

Smith, James K. A. *You Are What You Love: The Spiritual Power of Habit.* Grand Rapids: Brazos, 2016.

Spitzer, Robert. *New Proofs for the Existence of God: Contributions of Contemporary Physics and Philosophy.* Grand Rapids: Eerdmans, 2010.

Stonestreet, John. "Everybody Was Talking About Jesus Monday Night, Even Scott Van Pelt." Breakpoint, Jan. 23, 2025. https://breakpoint.org/everybody-was-talking-about-jesus-monday-night-even-scott-van-pelt/.

Stonestreet, John, and Kasey Leander. "You Don't Need to 'Gaslight Yourself.'" Breakpoint, Oct. 27, 2022. https://breakpoint.org/you-dont-need-to-gaslight-yourself/.

Strachan, Owen. *Reenchanting Humanity: A Theology of Mankind.* Ross-shire, UK: Mentor, 2019. Kindle.

Strauss, Mark. *Mark: Zondervan Exegetical Commentary on the New Testament.* Edited by Clinton Arnold. Grand Rapids: Zondervan, 2014. Kindle.

Strobel, Lee. *The Case for a Creator: A Journalist Investigates Scientific Evidence That Points Toward God.* Grand Rapids: Zondervan, 2004.

Taylor, Charles. *A Secular Age.* Cambridge, MA: Belknap, 2007.

Thielman, Frank. *The NIV Application Commentary: Philippians.* Grand Rapids: Zondervan, 1995.

Tolle, Eckhart. *The Power of Now: A Guide to Spiritual Enlightenment.* Novato, CA: New World Library; Vancouver, BC: Namaste Publishing, 1999.

Tripp, Paul. *Forever: Why You Can't Live Without It.* Grand Rapids: Zondervan, 2011. Kindle.

Trueman, Carl. *The Rise and Triumph of the Modern Self: Cultural Amnesia, Expressive Individualism, and the Road to Sexual Revolution.* Wheaton, IL: Crossway, 2020.

BIBLIOGRAPHY

———. *Strange New World: How Thinkers and Activists Redefined Identity and Sparked the Sexual Revolution*. Wheaton, IL: Crossway, 2022. Kindle.
Turley, Stephen. *Awakening Wonder: A Classical Guide to Truth, Goodness, and Beauty*. Camp Hill, PA: Classical Academic, 2014. Kindle.
Tutu, Desmond. *No Future Without Forgiveness*. New York: Doubleday, 1999. Kindle.
Vandrunen, David. *God's Glory Alone: The Majestic Heart of Christian Faith and Life*. Grand Rapids: Zondervan, 2015.
Villodas, Rich. *Good and Beautiful and Kind: Becoming Whole in a Fractured World*. Colorado Springs, CO: WaterBrook, 2022.
Volf, Miroslav. *Exclusion and Embrace: A Theological Exploration of Identity, Otherness, and Reconciliation*. Nashville: Abingdon, 2019. Kindle.
Watson, Thomas, and Jason Roth. *The Art of Divine Contentment: In Modern English*. Translation and annotations by Jason Roth. Christian Classics for the Modern Reader. Independently published, 2017. Kindle.
Weingarten, Gene. "Pearls Before Breakfast: Can One of the Nation's Great Musicians Cut Through the Fog of a D.C. Rush Hour? Let's Find Out." *Washington Post*, Apr. 8, 2007. https://www.washingtonpost.com/lifestyle/magazine/pearls-before-breakfast-can-one-of-the-nations-great-musicians-cut-through-the-fog-of-a-dc-rush-hour-lets-find-out/2014/09/23/8a6d46da-4331-11e4-b47c-f5889e061e5f_story.html.
Williams, Thaddeus. *Don't Follow Your Heart: Boldly Breaking the Ten Commandments of Self-Worship*. Grand Rapids: Zondervan Reflective, 2023. Kindle.

www.ingramcontent.com/pod-product-compliance
Lightning Source LLC
Chambersburg PA
CBHW071424160426
43195CB00013B/1792